MW01438518

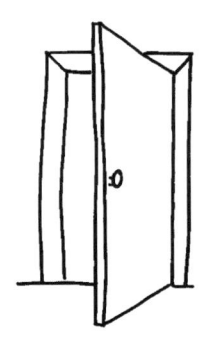

10 Days in February
... Limitations

Owning our story can be hard
but not nearly as difficult
as spending our lives running from it.
Embracing our vulnerabilities is risky
but not nearly as dangerous
as giving up on love and belonging and joy...
Only when we are brave enough
to explore the darkness
will we discover the infinite power of our light.
—*Dr. Brené Brown*

a memoir by
Eleanor Deckert
BOOK 3

10 Days in March
... Possibilities

Those who can, do.
Those who can do more, volunteer.
—Author Unknown

bright
dark
the cycle continues
Eleanor

a memoir by
Eleanor Deckert
BOOK 4

◆ FriesenPress

Suite 300 - 990 Fort St
Victoria, BC, Canada, V8V 3K2
www.friesenpress.com

Disclaimer: This content is not intended to be a substitute for professional medical advice, diagnosis, or treatment, and is a reflection of the author's experiences only.

Copyright © 2018 by Eleanor Deckert

Photo Credits:
Front Cover: Liz Guenther
Author Portrait: Kevin Deckert
Author as a child: school photo
Cabin: Fran McRae
Line drawings: Eleanor Deckert

✝ *Seven Predictable Patterns* ®

Reviews, photos, events, ordering info is found on author's web page.
www.eleanordeckert.com
All rights reserved.

No part of this publication may be reproduced in any form, or by any means, electronic or mechanical, including photocopying, recording, or any information browsing, storage, or retrieval system, without permission in writing from FriesenPress.

ISBN
978-1-5255-2993-1 (Hardcover)
978-1-5255-2994-8 (Paperback)
978-1-5255-2995-5 (eBook)

1. Biography & Autobiography, Personal Memoirs
2. Family & Relationships, Ethics & Morals
3. Self-Help, Green Lifestyle

Distributed to the trade by The Ingram Book Company

INVITATION

In an interesting creative experiment, Eleanor challenged herself to write Book 3 and Book 4 of her memoir by interlocking the 'Limitations' of midwinter in February with the 'Possibilities' of springtime activities in March.

In 1978, Eleanor and her newlywed husband, Kevin, built a tiny log cabin intending to live the 'Back-to-the-Land' lifestyle in the Canadian mountain wilderness. Eleanor chronicles a span of 40 years as they welcome new babies, improve their living conditions, and their dream becomes a reality.

Woven into the narrative are descriptions of her neighbours, community activities and the history of the tiny village of Avola, British Columbia.

Eleanor defines the month of February as 'the longest month of the year.' However, focusing on her experiences with depression does not result in gloom and melancholy. Rather, as she explores various resources and takes action towards personal wellness, this heartfelt memoir becomes inspirational.

In each of the chapters set during the month of March, Eleanor describes the volunteer activities that expand her world in ever widening circles. By volunteering, she increases her skills, builds friendships and improves her self-concept.

As in the other books in the series, Readers are invited to follow three levels in each chapter: The events of a specific day, the previous back-story, and the inner pathways of the Author's thoughts and feelings, doubts and beliefs.

A new feature at the end of each chapter is 'What Happened Next?' which fast-forwards the story to a satisfying conclusion.

DEDICATION
10 Days in February... Limitations

Who has listened to my story?
Who has observed my gloomy self-doubt?
Who is willing to walk with me
when I can barely walk myself?
Who offers a soothing word of wisdom,
comforting cup of tea, a warm blanket or a reassuring hug?

I am fortunate.
Both my Mother and my Husband
have had the patience and endurance
to listen while I grapple with February's depression.

ಸಿ ✿ ಲ
Gratitude To My Mother
Elisabeth
Who is willing to listen while I Journey.
ಸಿ ✿ ಲ

ಸಿ ✿ ಲ
Gratitude To My Husband
Kevin
Who provides stability
during Rocky, Stormy,
Foggy parts of my Path.
ಸಿ ✿ ಲ

DEDICATION
10 Days in March... Possibilities

Who has witnessed my creativity?
Who celebrates the essential, sacred
satisfaction of volunteering?
Who congratulates me
and remains dedicated to our relationship,
while encouraging me to explore, expand, and excel?

I am fortunate.
Both my Husband and my Mother
support me through the days, weeks, months,
even a full year of my time
pursuing personal goals as a volunteer.

ಐ ✿ ಜ

With Heartfelt Thanks To My Mother
Elisabeth
Who, in myriad ways,
has been an example of creativity and volunteering.

ಐ ✿ ಜ

ಐ ✿ ಜ

With Heartfelt Thanks To My Husband
Kevin
Who, with unfailing dedication,
volunteers as an Emergency Responder,
and has supported my volunteer efforts for over forty years.

ಐ ✿ ಜ

FOREWORD
10 Days in February... Limitations

I was honoured when Eleanor asked me to write this Foreword. Her previous books have been authentic, and this one also hits the mark.

Winter is a difficult time for some people, but when you experience depression it can be unbearable. I have suffered from Major Clinical Depression and SAD (Seasonal Affective Disorder) for most of my life. Once I was able to recognize the issue and get the help I needed, the fog began to lift and my world became, slowly, a brighter place.

I know from first hand experience the unrelenting fatigue, despair, anger and roller coaster of emotions that are part of living with this disease. Eleanor's descriptions of her days in February are evocative and are so reflective of my own worst days. She manages to accurately portray the feelings, thoughts and darkness that come with living with a mental illness.

Coping strategies are key to survival when you suffer from depression. I do not use the word 'suffer' casually. It is a dreadful disease, but when those of us diagnosed with depression are able to share our experiences and feelings we take one step closer to erasing the stigma that can be associated with mental illness.

Eleanor brings light, colour and hope back into her life of darkness and shares this experience honestly with her readers.

If you see yourself in the pages of this book, please seek medical attention. You do not need to suffer in silence, or alone.

Laura Soles
Clearwater, BC
June, 2018

FOREWORD
10 Days in March... Possibilities

There is a tremendous joy that comes from the voluntary, spontaneous 'doing' of 'something that needs doing.' This spirit of volunteerism is the thread that binds a group of diverse individuals together and little by little weaves the fabric of a community.

In my walk as a volunteer, I have discovered that unreserved, joyful giving is the catalyst that encourages others to believe in their own abilities and to join in.

This is the type of giving that we will find within the pages of this book.

A gift, however, is nothing if there is not another person to be the recipient of these gifts. Living with such limited resources, what does Eleanor have to give? Living in such a small community, who does she give to?

Indeed, as we embark on this journey with the author, we watch how the act of volunteering fuels the spark of life found deep within her, helping her to cope with the isolation, mundane chores and anxiety she also experienced in her homesteading lifestyle in rural Canada.

What motivates Eleanor? What motivates each of us, as we volunteer? The search for answers to this question is what this delightful book is all about.

Come. Share this part of Eleanor's Journey.

Cheryl Thomas, 2002 recipient of
Queen's Golden Jubilee
Medal Honouring Volunteers

Table of Contents
10 Days in February... Limitations

Invitation	v
Dedication	vi
Foreword	viii
Chapter 1 Friday, February 16, 1979	1
Chapter 2 Friday, February 26, 1982	35
Chapter 3 Wednesday, February 1, 1984	67
Chapter 4 Monday, February 9, 1987	89
Chapter 5 Saturday, February 16, 1991	117
Chapter 6 this year 'February' lasts from Christmas Eve, 1996...until May, 1997...a total of 139 days	143

Table of Contents
10 Days in March... Possibilities

Dedication	vii
Foreword	ix
Chapter 1 Thursday, March 22, 1979	21
Chapter 2 Tuesday, March 9, 1982	53
Chapter 3 Saturday, March 17, 1984	79
Chapter 4 Tuesday, March 31, 1987	105
Chapter 5 Monday, March 6, 1995	129
Chapter 6 Friday, March 21, 1997	159

Table of Contents... continued
10 Days in February... Limitations

Chapter 7
Tuesday, February 28, 2006　　　　173

Chapter 8
Tuesday, February 12, 2008　　　　201

Chapter 9
Sunday, February 6, 2011　　　　225

Chapter 10
Friday, February 9, 2018　　　　253

Table of Contents... continued
10 Days in March... Possibilities

Chapter 7
Tuesday, March 27, 2007   189

Chapter 8
Thursday, March 11, 2010   213

Chapter 9
Ash Wednesday, March 9, 2011   239

Chapter 10
Saturday, March 3, 2018   267

Endnotes   278

What Readers Are Saying   282

About The Author   283

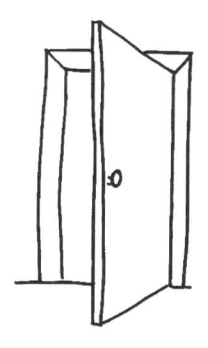

Chapter 1
Friday, February 16, 1979

What you can do,
or dream to do,
begin it.
—*Goethe*

↘↓↙

6:30
I was going to go. But, I decided to stay.

It's so hard to decide. There are pros and cons either way.

The days are so monotonous. The nights are so exhausting. The cold is so pervasive. The clock ticks so slowly. The calendar is so heavy. 'Cabin Fever' is so real. Two people in such a small space is such a strain.

Any change would be welcome. But, I decided to stay.

I was going to go with Kevin. He goes every Friday. I already know how his day will go. Walk two miles to the highway. Hitchhike ten miles to town. Walk two more miles to Fran and Archie's place. Welcome. People. Food. Bath. Telephone. News. Laughter. Warmth. Laundry. That's a lot of 'pros' to look forward to.

But, I decided to stay. Recently, the warmer temperatures brought heavy snowfall. That will make the walk out slow and tiring. Last night the temperature dropped again. If I go, too, the fire will be out. The cabin will be frigid by the time we get home.

I am tired of the isolation. Even more than that, I am *so* tired of the cold. I am so *tired* of the cold. I am so tired of the *cold*. So, even in exchange for a day of friends and feasting, I really don't want to return to face an empty wood stove, my water jar frozen solid, my mattress colder than a deep-freeze.

"Be safe!" With a hug, I mutter into his down parka.

My heart tugs as I watch my husband disappear into the winter white, early morning, darkness.

I blow a kiss and whisper, "Come back."

↘↓↙

So, the day begins. A three layered day. I will imagine where Kevin is as the hours go by. I will accomplish my daily tasks. I will amuse myself, or battle, with my own inner thoughts.

"It's just us now," I stroke Ember, our kitten, wrapped in my arms. I look into the eyes of Sam, our German shepherd. They can't help saw, carry, split or stack firewood. They can't help scoop, dump, melt or filter the snow into water. They can't help peel or dice the last of the frozen potatoes, nor measure and simmer the daily ration of beans. They can't eek out the remaining supplies. But, somehow, their continuous company, entertaining antics, unwavering trust, and reliable protection build my courage for the day ahead and relieve me of the weight of solitary silence while I wait, hoping for Kevin's safe return.

Friday, February 16, 1979

Turning from the window, I open the wood cook stove, feed quarters of birch into the flames and pour a cup of mint tea, my only luxury. It's a little before 7:00. I blow out the kerosene lamp. The sky gets lighter earlier now. Midwinter darkness is slowly rolling back.

"O, Canada," I sigh.

Outdoors with all of my pots and pans, I scoop snow, pressing it down, return to the cabin and set them on the stove to melt for dish water. Meanwhile, I can sweep the bare wood floor.

Since I married a Canadian, I voluntarily live much further north than the Colorado mountains I loved in my childhood. Inspired by the commitment to family I had read in the 'Little House on the Prairie' books, Kevin and I chose the 'Back-to-the Land' lifestyle. I voluntarily experience the limitations and challenges, eager to learn the skills. I have so much to learn.

My parents, like millions of others born in the 1930s, married in the 1950s and raised my four siblings and I through the 1960s. With our two-car garage and middle-income, suburban, 'white picket fence' lifestyle, they could give their children every convenience they did not have.

Now Kevin and I, like thousands of others in the 1970s, have deliberately walked away from a college education, women's lib, two pay cheques, TV, status symbols of all kinds, consumerism.

Retracing the path that led to this moment, I recall our Ontario outdoor wedding on a daisy-filled June morning, driving across the prairies in our red and white VW van, camping along the way, exploring the mountains and valleys of British Columbia, believing that the God of the Universe was somehow interested in the details guiding our decisions.

We had only $40 left when we pulled into Avola, and we had only one reason to stop there. We had put an advertisement in the 'Natural Life' magazine[1] stating our intention to start a homestead in the mountains, and we noticed a letter in the magazine which described just what we were looking for! Fran wrote the letter to encourage young people looking for the 'Self-Sufficient' lifestyle to consider restoring the old cabins and coaxing the land back to productivity. Fran and Archie, a retired couple with decades of practical experience, took us to look at land, offered their generous hospitality while we built our log cabin, and encouraged us every step of the way. We came to rely on them.

We found land in August, in the North Thompson River valley, just south of Avola. Howard, the owner of the land, accepted the down payment of $1000.[2] Standing dead timber provided the logs Kevin would wrestle into place to build our first home. Working as a waitress at a truck stop in Avola, I brought in the cash we needed for food, gas, lumber for the floor and roof, spikes, roofing paper, tar and hinges.

We moved into our tiny, uninsulated log cabin on December 22.[3] All throughout November and December, the temperature had been mild, a little above and a little below freezing. The Old Timers told Tall Tales of the oncoming cold weather, but they seemed like an exaggeration to me.

But, I was wrong.

On December 28, during the night, the temperature suddenly dropped. Minus 40°C was a shock. Our van froze up. Without a vehicle to get to town, I lost my job. The gaps between the floorboards sucked in Arctic breezes. The only source of heat was the wood cook stove with a firebox only a little bigger than a shoe box! Even when we carefully fit in the maximum amount of firewood, the flames reduced to coals in one-and-a-half hours.

Every night, to survive the bitter cold, we had to set the wind-up alarm clock and take turns climbing down the ladder from the sleeping loft. My head ached from interrupted sleep.

Friday, February 16, 1979

Again and again. Night after icy night. It felt like torture to maintain the fire.

Every day, Kevin watched the clock, turning on the radio only for the news. He did not want to waste the batteries.

"Three weeks. That's how long this cold spell is expected to last."

Facts. Reality smashed against my pleasant idealistic dreams. Newlyweds! Homesteading! My imagination had provided a very cozy view anticipating our first winter. We would be so cheerful with our well stocked pantry, so comfortable in our cabin, two romantic sweethearts enjoying new experiences.

But, it has been so very extremely, dangerously cold. In January, 1979, the temperatures were 20°C colder than average. The cold spell lasted a record 26 days. The only good thing about it was the bright, clear sunshine.

Vicious. That's the word! January. I'm glad that's over.

February is different. What a relief to have milder temperatures at last. But, with the warmer temperature comes cloudy, grey, overcast skies. Snowfall this month has really added up. Kevin shovelled the soft, fresh snow to bank up against the lower part of the cabin. That stopped the drafts. It really helped.

Yesterday the temperature dropped. It's 'only' minus 15°C. The sky finally cleared. We could see the sun! Good-bye dreary grey! The sky is bright! There is more light in the cabin.

Still, no, thank-you. I don't want to be out in the cold, nor return to an icy stove.

↘↓↙

8:00

So, here I am.

"The only difference between what he's wearing and what I'm wearing is the backpack," I explain to the kitten. I wear long johns and my flannel PJ pants inside my black men's wool work pants, two layers of wool socks inside my felt-pack boots, four layers of sweaters (one cotton, three wool) and my down parka, wool scarf and hat. Yes, indoor gear and outdoor gear are about the same when the temperature drops.

By now, Kevin is probably crossing the bridge over the frozen river and climbing the hill to the highway, I imagine.

The pot of snow has melted on the stove now and the water is hot enough for the dishpan.

"I hope he gets a ride," I mumble to the kitten. "It's so cold to stand there waiting, hoping."

That's one of the reasons I didn't want to go. Whenever I hitchhike, I end up feeling so grumpy. The longer I stand there, the more miserable my tumbling thoughts. "Hey, you! Stop and help us! It's cold out here! We aren't doing this for fun! We aren't planning an attack! Just give us a warm ride... Please!" I lose faith in the goodness of my fellow man! That feels like its own kind of cold.

The cabin is tidy now. It only takes a few minutes.

He must be in Avola by now. It only takes a few minutes.

"He'll have to walk the two miles to Fran and Archie's house. I might as well do my outdoor chores now." Sam bounds out the door and begins his route, sniffing here and there. I call it 'reading the newspaper.' He makes his rounds and joins me as I split kindling at the chopping block.

Kevin and I went out in the forest recently, looking for the places Kevin had left stacks of wood.

Kevin cut the logs for our house with a double-bitted axe and a one man crosscut saw.[4] After building the cabin three logs high in the traditional way, he paused and realized that working alone would be dangerous the higher he went. If he used short, upright logs, they would be light and he could carry them on his shoulder. Everything would move more

Friday, February 16, 1979

quickly. He measured and cut the upright lengths. He left piles of cedar here and there which were too short, or broken, or too small in diameter. So, today, I can load up the sled, pull the load, split what I have gathered and stack it against the cabin near the door.

It has been 55 days since we moved in. I have experience now. I can estimate how much wood will be needed for several days. I bring enough wood inside for today and tonight. Some is cedar, split small to restart the fire on the glowing coals. Some is birch, very valuable for its long lasting heat. Some is the mill end lumber Fran and Archie's son, Red, brought from the sawmill where he works. The mill ends are mostly spruce and fir which throws a good heat for cooking and baking.

I interrupt firewood chores frequently to refill the pots and pans with snow every time they melt down.

Feed the dog. Feed the cat.

I have had to improve the cat's litter box. We ran out of kitty litter long ago. Buying food was more important. The bitter cold made the plastic box brittle so it shattered. I improvised a cardboard box lined with a garbage bag and I found a place where the road cut through a gravel bank. I can scrape dirt into the box. The cat seems to think that it's OK. The freezing temperature inside during the cold spell reduced the stink.

Next, pour the dish water into the slop-water bucket and dump it down the slop-pit. Dump the chamber pot into the outhouse.

"That's all for today," I announce in case the cat and dog are listening.

By now, Kevin is enjoying a hearty breakfast at Fran and Archie's farm kitchen table. Hot porridge cooled with goat's milk is followed by scrambled eggs from their chickens. Homemade bread is toasted and several pots of jam bring summer's bounty to the winter mornings.

I bring water to a boil, stir in a handful of rolled oats, sprinkle on a few raisins and take inventory of our dwindling supplies. Our last trip to town for groceries was December 30th. Although we spent almost every penny on food, making thrifty vegetarian choices, no prepared food, mostly ingredients, only a few canned goods, $300 can only stretch so far. Now only flour, oatmeal, potatoes, some powdered milk and oil, peanut butter, a little brown sugar, cinnamon and raisins are left. Oh, and soy sauce and a little ketchup. "Not much of a menu," I mumble, trying to figure out how to make meals from this. From the start, we decided to only eat twice a day. We stayed in bed so much during the bitter cold. The winter nights were so long and the daylight so short, there was no need for a midday meal.

10:00

Only three hours have passed since Kevin left. I look at the calendar. I have been making an X on each day. First, each day so bitterly cold. Then, each day so dreary and grey. Suddenly an idea flashes in my mind. I take a pen and make today's X. Then fill in one quarter with another smaller X. "There. Now I can measure every time three hours passes." Somehow that feels like an achievement. I can cross off three long hours, four times within each long day. Each day is a part of this longest month. This month is a part of this longest season. Without anything to look forward to, no goals, only the monotony of the day's routine, the scarce food supplies measured out into two meals per day, the endless battle against the cold, the lack of human companionship, laughter, hugs or stimulation for the intellect, I am just treading water in a boundaryless ocean. Endlessly.

Except when I read.

Friday, February 16, 1979

While Kevin does whatever he is doing up there in Avola, I load wood into the cook stove and the small wood heater that Howard brought on the last day of December. Grateful for this one major improvement, now we can sleep for four hours before refilling the stove. I set my boots near the stove to dry, hang up my parka, climb the ladder, and nestle into my sleeping bag with a book.

↘↓↙

So far this winter I have nourished my mind and escaped the harsh limitations by reading several classics. My Mother mailed 21 cases of my belongings to me while we built our cabin. Several cases were books! 'Wuthering Heights' and 'Jane Eyre' were so dreary; grey moors, moaning wind, spooky mansions, lonely characters. 'Robinson Crusoe' seemed more lively, but he lived in complete isolation, too, surviving and improvising solutions to problems. Then he found a wild man he named 'Friday' and had human companionship, but it took years for him to return to civilization. The theme of isolation also knit together 'Gulliver's Travels' as he explored various fantasy civilizations. Once Gulliver was a giant. In another place he was very tiny in comparison to the local inhabitants he found. 'Swiss Family Robinson' brought family togetherness into the mix, but still, they were cut off from the rest of the world. They built. They set up food supplies. They defended themselves. They thrived.

Fran has also been lending us books from her collection on ecological topics. 'Robots Behind the Plow' points out the threats of industrial farming. Rachel Carson's 'Silent Spring' warns of how the use of DDT and other chemicals in farming may be bringing, not the intended abundance, but may actually be slowly destroying fertility.

February Chapter 1

Kevin and I have also attempted an orderly reading of the Bible. By reading it straight through, I can see a pattern. God calls. The person says 'Yes.' Then challenges begin. The person is alone. How to endure? Doubt? Believe? Finally God's promise comes true. I never noticed the hard part before. As a child in Sunday School, I only noticed the obedience and that 'the good guy' gets to the end.

I also have books from my childhood. 'Charlotte's Web' warms my heart with seasonal scenes, family familiarity, ingenious imagination. 'Little Princess' builds my endurance as Sarah faces hardship and retains her courage. E. Nesbit describes family adventures which stretches my belief in a bright future with our own children. C.S. Lewis weaves allegory into the fantasy world he creates with his pen. Fairy tales contain lessons and always resolution. The happy ending comes after the hero or heroine trusts a Helper or Stranger, an Old Woman or Little Man.

And I most certainly trust the One who I believe is Guiding us on our Life Path.

Today, I choose an old textbook of poetry. I can flip the pages and find thought provoking and encouraging treasures.

Some say the world will end in fire.
Some say in ice...
Robert Frost

Without Divine assistance
I cannot succeed;
with it I cannot fail.
Abraham Lincoln

Friday, February 16, 1979

Within a few pages I doze off in the warmth and security of my sleeping bag.

↘↓↙

12:00 noon

I just awoke from a marvellous dream. The kind when you see faces and colours and hear cheerful voices and even music. I could peer around corners and looked closely at details.

It all began when I was walking past a building that had been empty for many years, cold and dark, silent and grey.

But, to my surprise, there were several cars parked and people entering the open door.

I stepped in. Where previously there had been hollow echoes, sagging cobwebs and stale memories, I was amazed to see a fully furnished room. In the centre was a large, dark, old-fashioned desk. Glass-door cabinets held colourful displays of marionettes and dolls from around the world. Benches along the window had welcoming, colourful cushions. Shelves burst with brightly bound books. On counter tops, oversized books beckoned the passer-by to stop and look at pictures of far off places, animals, nature's wonders and craft ideas.

Art supplies on a low table invited children to participate. A basket of rhythm instruments looked intriguing. Blocks for babies. Crayons for tots. An easel with paint brushes waited for a creative hand.

I saw young children enjoying time with their mother's help and encouragement. I saw young mothers being encouraged by the older women, nodding and sharing. They discovered that they had so much in common.

I turned a corner and smelled coffee and muffins and I heard the chuckling, storytelling voices of older gentlemen.

Their grins and gestures showed how much they liked to get together.

Through another doorway I heard gentle music. I stepped into a carpeted room with a semicircle of comfy sofas and beanbag chairs facing a red brick fireplace. What was this? Young adults were singing together. I recognized familiar tunes and words from those 'we can make the world a better place to be' songs from the '60s and '70s. Harmonies met and shifted. Contentment and satisfaction was like a web interconnecting these people.

Back to the main room I asked the employee how this all came to be? What is this place of marvels, where the elderly and the youngest find activities, learning, and a sense of belonging?

It seemed to be such a place of wealth: maps and music, puzzles and games, pillows and paintings. A willing attendant was ready to help each patron follow his or her interest. I sensed an eager attitude of curious exploration and the thrill of the search.

Each person who entered shifted the group as they added their voice. Each person who left wore a smile. Each parent made the effort. Each child made a memory. Each of the elderly felt they had made a contribution. Each of the young had found a hub to go out from and return to.

Then I woke up and I knew. It was a library.

Hold on to this dream. These places exist. I cannot get there now. I can only remember the past and hope for the future. In the present, I can only imagine such places of abundance, learning and culture.

↘↓↙

Music, too, is in my imagination every day and through the long winter's night.

Friday, February 16, 1979

I don't care for the radio's percussive announcers nor the unpleasant news of the outside world. I don't need the high pitched electric guitar music. I have plenty of music in my head. And I can change to different tunes in an instant.

I played the clarinet for church on Christmas Eve, in parades with a marching band, for graduations and weddings and in the school band. When Kevin and I decided to head out west and live in the wilderness, I sold my clarinet.

I was in a musical called 'Where's Charlie' in my senior year of high school. 'Brigadoon' and 'Fiddler on the Roof,' and 'My Fair Lady' and 'West Side Story' were my other favourite musical plays. I suppose now that I live so far from a town, I will never participate in a theatre group.

I learned to play the guitar so I could sing John Denver songs of the wilderness, the good life, a country home, lasting love and nature's beauty. However, I don't know any songs that could have prepared me for the hardship and cold and crushing isolation. Hymns from church offered hope, but they also reminded me of how far away I am from fellowship.

Daddy had a vast record collection of classical music. Mother played the piano daily. Music was as much a daily part of family life as saying the Blessing at the supper table.

Still curled up in my sleeping bag, I try to find a melody in my memory to soothe my longing heart. But, instead of a richly textured orchestra, my mind supplies a tune which demonstrates how I really feel right now. It's Lamb Chop with the world's most annoying repetitive *This is the song that never ends...* Oh, No! Please! Can I turn the dial in my mind and find something a little more nourishing? TV ads pop up: 'coo-coo for Cocoa Puffs,' 'I am the Frito Bandito' then 'N-e-s-t-l-e-s. Nestle's makes the very best... chocolate.' Now the theme music from TV shows: 'The Bionic Woman,' 'Little House on the Prairie,' 'Gilligan's Island,' and 'The Beverly Hillbillies.'[5]

Pushing these away, at last Kermit's soothing voice brings me *It's not that easy being green...* and I commiserate with him, and come to his resolution, *I am green. It's beautiful. And it's what I want to be.*

Is this what I want to be?

Sigh.

↘↓↙

Returning from my literary longings and musical musings, leaving my cozy dreams, my senses signal reality. I climb back down the ladder. For the zillionth time, I feed the fire, strain the clean water, scoop more snow.

While Kevin is in town, I hope he phones both of our families. My family has not communicated at all recently. I keep worrying. However, Kevin's Mom has been very steady in her pledge to mail us a $20 check once a month for the first year as a wedding gift. Last week, birthday money also arrived for Kevin. We had to spend it on high priorities: a 50 pound bag of dog food (the cat eats this, too), a two gallon jug of kerosene and batteries for the radio. These were not exactly birthday presents! Our grocery shopping had to be whatever was the least money for the most meals: potatoes, oats, rice, beans.

As he does every week, I'm sure Kevin will phone the railroad office to ask for a job. He will also go to the post office. I guess I am like Pollyanna. No matter the limitations or the circumstances, there is always hope. Fran will probably give him a loaf of bread. Maybe some eggs.

I scrape the sides of the bucket of honey, saving every drop into a smaller glass jar. I reheat some soup. Childhood family rules prompt me to wash my hands before I eat, say the Blessing before food is served, put my napkin on my lap.

Friday, February 16, 1979

"May I be excused?" I ask the cat and clear off my place at the table.

1:00
Time to cross off another quarter space on the calendar with an X, check the fire, and climb back up to the sleeping loft.

Spending the afternoon in my sleeping bag, I imagine the past, escape from the present and reach towards the future. One thing I have learned this winter. My mind is stronger than my body. My dreams are stronger than this reality. When I wish I was someplace else, I can concentrate and recreate people, places, sounds, conversations and collect details to treasure. In the reality of this poverty, I can escape.

Another nap. Another hour of dozing, remembering, imagining.

↘↓↙

Someday, I'll have a granddaughter. Someday, she'll ask me, "Grammie, tell me the story of your life."

Someday, I'll tell her how my heart jumped when I first saw Grampa Kevin! We were both sixteen years old! How handsome he was standing in the snowy sunshine, his khaki canvas coat open, his curly black hair tossed in the breeze. I'll tell her about tobogganing, and hot dog roasts, and snowshoes, and target practice. I'll tell her what movies we went to, and how Kevin built my Mother a chicken barn, and helped my Grandfather during the blizzard. I'll tell her how Kevin peddled 500 miles on a bicycle to get to college. I'll tell her how we held hands and sweetly gave each other a good-night kiss, how we lay in the tall grass planning to go out west, how we sat on the pebbly beach beside the river and planned our log cabin, how we walked through the forest and planned our children and customs, and how we waited until we were 20 years old to get married outdoors under God's blue sky, in God's wonderful Creation, on a daisy-filled morning with muffins and fruit salad and grape juice to serve our guests.

Someday, I'll describe everything to her: the red and white VW van we set up to camp in, the whispering pines swishing in the wind as we slept in Ontario, the hail beating down in Manitoba, the sunflower acres in Saskatchewan, the rhythm of the bobbing oil rigs in Alberta, the way my heart began to sing when I saw the towering snow-capped peaks in British Columbia. I'll tell her how, with the help of Fran and Archie, we found our land when we had only $40 left. I'll describe how Kevin built the cabin, alone, with hand tools, solving problems, being safe, working through the rain and frosty mornings while I was a waitress at the Avola truck-stop.

Someday, when I tell her about this first bitterly cold winter it will sound like a story of adventure, courage and endurance.

Someday, I won't be cold, and alone, and rationing kerosene, eating monotonous meals every day, waiting, wondering.

Someday, I won't be focused on trying not to be afraid.

Someday, today will be yesterday.

I wonder if I will tell my granddaughter that sometimes there seemed to be icebergs between my husband and I. As if the cold and isolation was not enough, we fell into silence, locked in disagreements or feeling offended, unable to redirect communication, untangle misunderstandings or re-state an opinion in a quieter tone of voice. Kevin only has one brother ten years older, so it is as if he is an only child. He has very little practice resolving differences. I am quick with words, quick with alternatives, quick in a way that makes him feel overwhelmed and dizzy. When he shuts off communication, I can't figure out what he expects from me as a wife. His mother was widowed when Kevin was only thirteen. Maybe he doesn't have much experience observing married couples.

Sometimes I wonder, like I did in December: Stay? or Go?

But then, after a few bewildering attempts at reconciliation, we both seem to turn an important corner and both seem more cheerful, more industrious, more civil to each other, more hopeful of the future. We both resolve to become more strong and dependable, to listen, to monitor tone of voice.

And then, once again, I melt into the security of my husband's embrace.

↘↓↙

4:00

It is almost time to X off the third quarter of this day on the calendar square. Almost 4:00. Almost evening. Almost time to wonder when Kevin will be home.

More wood. More water. More waiting.

And then the dog barks. Bounding out, he hears Kevin whistle.

My husband is home! I didn't realize how tense I was while waiting.

Stomping off his boots, swinging his backpack down, stepping to the stove to warm his hands, Kevin returns. News. Mail. Books. Clean laundry. Fran sent a loaf of white bread, a jar of jam, a dozen eggs. And, wonder and marvellous, look! His heavy backpack is full of split peas!

"There was a truck accident near Avola and the cargo spilled. People went to shovel up the split peas to take home to feed their chickens, pigs and horses. Then, Mrs. Buis at the post office reminded the gleaners that we were vegetarians. So, they saved some for us!"

"It will fill the bucket I cleaned out from the last of the honey!" I am so happy to see so much food. "Look! It will fill the gallon jar, too, and maybe even this ketchup can!"

Kevin lights the lamp.

"Let's have French Toast for supper!" I quickly set the cast iron frying pan over the flames, stir powdered milk into the eggs, dip the bread and enjoy the golden smell. I put the plates into the warming shelf so the food will stay hot when it is served.

While we savour the toast and jam, he tells all he heard, saw and experienced. "Cheryl wants to know if you will come and babysit for a few days in mid-March." Cheryl is Archie's daughter. Cheryl and her husband, Jim, live with their two young children, Bonnie and Jack, in the large farmhouse on Fran and Archie's property, leaving the house trailer to the older couple.

"Oh! Yes!" Something to look forward to. I glance at the calendar. Only five weeks away.

We blow out the lamp as soon as possible and wait in our sleeping bags until 9:00 to turn on the radio play. KIRO, the Seattle station features a western, mystery, romance, drama or comedy every week night. Andy Griffith is the host on Fridays for the comedy.

We giggle in the dark.

Warm weather has replaced the worst of the winter. Anticipating days ahead to interact with the children has greatly lifted my spirits. I realize that somehow I think I will make it through February!

What Happened Next?

I continued to mark the large X on each day of the calendar, filling in each quarter every three hours. The days continued

Friday, February 16, 1979

long, repetitive and uneventful. The food supplies were so diminished that for the rest of February and most of March our two meals a day were reduced even further.

For breakfast you could have oatmeal with either brown sugar *or* raisins *or* cinnamon.

For supper you could have split peas with either ketchup *or* onions *or* soy sauce.

The Past, the Present and the Future battle inside me. I had decided to leave behind the abundance, ease and shelter of living in the Church Community in Ontario. I dream and reach ahead towards the day when our homestead will produce our water, food and fuel supply. I eagerly anticipate children and family adventures while they learn and grow. But, in the Here and Now, the bleak emptiness, interrupted only by repetition to supply bare necessities, this was my reality.

Silently, I was in a state of continual strain, whispering, shouting, begging, whining, "I wish I was someplace else!"

I became aware of any little pleasure: the cheerful call of the chickadees. I savoured any little comfort: the dancing flames warming my outstretched hands. I paused to appreciate any little beauty: the sunlight glinting through the icicles on the eves. I rehearsed the pledges and vows and promises Kevin and I had made to each other and re-stated my goals: "I want to get married, go out west, build a log cabin, raise a bunch of kids, teach them about the Lord, volunteer in my community, and then write a book about it."

I wrote one page in my Journal each month. I preserved details which confirmed that, indeed, no matter how desperate I felt, there was evidence that Someone was helping us, Guiding, Directing, Providing.

Fear was there, but Trust won the battle.

Praise God from Whom all blessings flow!

Indelible experiences in February, 1979.

Chapter 1
Thursday, March 22, 1979

> How wonderful it is
> that nobody need wait a single moment
> before starting to improve the world.
> —Anne Frank

↖↑↗

"I'm so happy!"

Every gesture and stride is energetic as Kevin and I hike the two miles to the highway. Cheryl is coming to pick us up. Sam wags his tail and bounds ahead. Ember has a heap of food left for her in the cabin. We are going to Avola for five whole days and four whole nights. And, better than the warm house, electric light, running water and use of the telephone, she has asked me to babysit! I get to play with their two preschoolers, Bonnie and Jack, while Jim and Cheryl have a little holiday at the coast, quick before Baby #3 arrives in the spring!

March Chapter 1

ĸ↑↗

Last time I was in Avola, when I had hitchhiked up with Kevin on a brisk Friday in late February, I hadn't been very cheerful.

"Every day is the same..." I moaned and sighed and leaned against the farmhouse kitchen counter.

Cheryl, as usual, had a zillion things to do and her rapidly moving hands were kneading the dough for eight loaves of bread. The washer and dryer were running, soup was simmering, the kids were done their TV show and starting to pester each other.

"Cut it out!" she shouted, "Get your snow pants on! We're going out to do the chores!"

She covered the dough with a clean towel and set the huge bowl up on top of the refrigerator. With the wood stove heating the place and warm air rising, it was the perfect temperature for the dough to rise. She quickly washed her hands, grabbed her work coat which no longer closed against her pregnant belly, and stepped into her rubber boots. I worked at pushing the children's boots on and got myself ready while Cheryl hustled Bonnie and Jack out the door. In one hand she had a bucket of hot soapy water. In the other she had the empty milk pail.

I tagged along. I felt foolish to be so glum. Yet, my droopy, heavy posture showed how real the 'February Blues' were for me. Cheryl scooped oats and the two milk goats were let out of their enclosure. They knew the routine. First Snowy White stepped up onto the milking stand to enjoy her feed of oats. Her head passed through the gap and Cheryl closed the latch to keep her steady while she milked. Efficiently, Cheryl wrung the cloth and washed the teats, brushing away loose hairs. Left-right-left-right, her thumb and first finger closed up near the udder and she squeezed her fingers to press the milk down and out.

I tried it a few times, but my slow, clumsy movement did not accomplish as much as her steady, experienced rhythm, so I seldom offered to 'help.' I scooped grain for the chickens and dumped the kitchen scrap bucket in for them to scratch and peck for goodies. My mind supplied a memory of Wilbur in 'Charlotte's Web' enjoying the bread crusts, a bit of carrot peal, a couple of apple cores and the scraping from the morning porridge pot. Until my husband and I arrived in Avola six months ago, I only knew about 'life on the farm' from reading books. And books don't convey the smells, mud, noises, or the hurry of the day to attend to so many tasks.

Bonnie was holding the basket for eggs. Black, red and white hens clucked quietly when, speaking coaxingly, she slowly, gently slid her little hand under each hen to feel for the warm, smooth eggs. Jack, quicker and less concerned with his 'nest-side-manner' felt competitive with his older sister and boldly announced, "I got a blue one!" Both of them knew to avoid the rooster. Bonnie hesitated and flashed a begging look to me. There was one black hen with a fancy speckled ruff who always pecked.

I discovered that she was setting on four eggs which her sisters had already laid. I slid my hand in under the fluffy, warm feathers again just to be sure I got them all.

Now Daisy stepped up onto the milking stand. It was built like a little deck for the goats to walk up onto so who ever was milking didn't have to crouch or squat down.

Cheryl made it all look so easy.

I wonder if these scenes are in my future? Someday it will be me, doing chores out in the barn, teaching the children, punching down the bread, feeding the fire, ladling homemade soup into bowls.

March Chapter 1

ᚴ↑↗

That dreary February day, I did not tell Cheryl the full reality of my situation. I didn't want her to feel sorry for me. I had already heard the other women at the restaurant advise me. "I would leave him." They didn't understand. They thought Kevin was making me do it. They didn't realize that I wanted this adventure. I wanted to experience something hard. My life in the Church Community had been so sheltered. Would what I believed be enough to see me through hard times? My life as the daughter of a university professor had been so sheltered. Would what I had been taught be of any use in this situation? Compared to almost anyone in history or around the world, my life had been so sheltered. Others live without running water, electricity, cars, telephones, can I do it, too? I wanted to know how I would endure, how I would behave, how it would feel. Would I ever get hungry enough to 'steal a loaf of bread?' Would my mental health, or marriage, or morals crumble?

Oatmeal.
Split peas.
Kerosene.
Firewood.
Water.
Sleeping bag.
Crossing off the calendar every three hours,
four times each day.
That was my life for most of February.
Limitations.

Thursday, March 22, 1979

↖↑↗

But, today, the world seems full of possibilities! It's the Spring Equinox! The daylight comes so much earlier and lasts so much longer! Miracle of miracles: the daytime temperature is above freezing!

"Kevin, do you realize how happy I am!" I like to tell him what I'm thinking as we trudge along the snowy road. "I first started babysitting when I was twelve years old. Some families call me 'Mary Poppins!' I've been counting: I have provided fun activities for more than 80 children! Five whole days with little kids! Bliss!"

Kevin looks at his watch as we approach the top of the slope and see the highway. "One of these next vehicles will be her!" He sounds cheerful, too.

Cheryl pulls up. The car is warm. The kids are excited. The miles zip by. February is o-v-e-r. March holds hope.

The children love to run to me, to be scooped up and swung in a circle when we arrive in the big, log farmhouse.

I have done overnight babysitting many times before we moved here. Kevin will be staying, too. I feel confident that we will have a wonderful time. Cheryl shows me things I will need to know.

Wood heater, wood cook stove, propane stove, washing machine, dryer, these I have already used on previous visits. Snowsuits, high chair, bath habits, favourite toys and books, pets, houseplants, telephone messages, emergency contacts, barn chores are all familiar. Of course, the grandparents, Fran and Archie, are only a few steps away in their house trailer, but they find the children's fast pace too energetic.

Cheryl's two brothers and their friend will be coming home from the sawmill at about 4:00pm. They bunk up in the attic. They expect me to make supper, but they make their own coffee, breakfast and lunch. Sounds like I will be washing a lot of dishes.

Cheryl shows me the well-stocked pantry, the garden-filled freezer, the root cellar lined with shelves of home-canned fruit, jams, pickles and baskets of potatoes, carrots, beets and squash. She already made the eight loaves of bread for the weekend. I plan to make muffins and bake cookies with the children 'helping' me measure and mix, sift and sample.

The children are too old for naps, too young for chores. They are quick to climb on the furniture, and have eyes teasing me to come and play. Bonnie is either very shy, or a little chatterbox. Jack is either in continual motion, or sound asleep. I will be busy!

Kevin and I will share the spare room just off the living room with a sheet tacked up for a little privacy.

Jim arrives home after a day of working on the railroad, showers and packs the car. The kids get big hugs. And they are off. The children finish waving until the car is out of sight. Jim and Cheryl will be back Monday afternoon.

Cheryl had already made the supper. Then comes a flurry of bedtime routines.

Thankfully, everyone sleeps through the first night.

↖↑↗

"Let's play hide-and-go-seek," I suggest.

While I count, Jack dives behind the couch. His blond hair and wide-open eyes peek out. Bonnie scoots under the bench beside the dining room table. She is curled up tight. Her eyes shut. If she can't see me, maybe I can't see her? "Is he behind the curtain?... No... Is she under the chair?... No... Are they in the closet?" I slowly search and they giggle and squirm. "O, I see you!" and we begin again. I had forgotten that little ones like to repeat everything. Although I searched high and low, Bonnie and Jack both hid in their same places, every time, all weekend!

"Do you know how to play 'Go Fish'?" I reduce the deck by half. I lay out the cards to see if they can read the numbers? Can they count? We play an 'open hand.' All the cards are face up so I can help them decide what to say and do. Bonnie helps Jack count. Jack is concentrating. Bonnie lays her pairs out end-to-end. Jack bounces when he gets a match.

No more holding still. We bring out the blocks and build and knock down towers. Bridges and forts, roadways and towers, racing quickly and slowly careful, there are so many variations. Kevin sees the fun and goes out to the woodworking shop. He knows there is a bin of scraps. In a little while, he returns with newly cut and sanded blocks: long and thin, wide and thick, little funny shapes, triangles. What fun we will have!

When the interest lags, I see some trucks and we zoom around the floor making "brummmm" sounds and beeping and honking the horns. Jack likes to crash. I like to deliver. Bonnie likes to explore.

The sun is setting behind the mountains. After so much activity, I think a quiet time would re-balance the children before we begin the evening routines. Bringing a blanket from my bed to cover the table and stretch across the chairs, I construct a tent. We add pillows, cuddly toys and books and build a nest. It is surprising how long an active child will stay quiet and calm within a cozy den. We look at pictures and talk about the animals, retell the stories, laugh at the silly illustrations, wonder what happens next.

Kevin has been peeling potatoes. Cheryl left a big meatloaf ready to pop into the oven. I search the freezer for vegetables from the garden. I run to the cellar for two jars of peaches. Well, maybe three. I scramble eggs and melt cheese for Kevin and I. We're vegetarians.

March Chapter 1

I have made it a habit to include children in chores, meal preparations, pet care and other 'grown-up' activities while I am taking care of them. It is my observation that routines, repetition, mimicking and rituals are very important to young children. It is, after all, how they learn to speak, get dressed and practice every other self-care skill. In my experience, children are pleased to be asked to help. I invite them with a suggestion. "Bonnie, would you like to wash the potatoes?" I tie a yellow apron around her. She stands on a chair and lifts the potatoes out of the cold water rinse and puts them into the pot. "Jack, are you strong enough to carry this?" I give Jack what we need for the table and he trots back and forth with silverware, napkins, salt and pepper, and one plate at a time.

Tomorrow, I will bring them both out to do chores in the barn, carry the firewood, sweep up the bits of bark, and crack the eggs, wait for the toast to pop and spread their own jam. However well or poorly children complete each task, it seems to me that they can learn if we do them together. It is not so that I have less work to do. The benefit to me is that the children stay close by, are attentive to my instructions, build trust in my leadership, are eager to please and realize that learning valuable skills is more fun than being dismissed to "Go play."

I hear the trucks in the driveway. I hear the clatter of firewood filling the wood box. The men come stomping in.

Jack is in his highchair. Bonnie is on the bench. The meal is ready. Chairs pulled into place, reaching hands, passing bowls, voices overlapping, stories and news interrupting. What a different scene from the silent two-person meals that Kevin and I have had in our cabin.

After supper, all hands clear the table. I wash up. Kevin stays to help. The other men pass around beer, turn on the TV and find sports to watch. The children run and jump, climb and pester, wanting attention.

In an attempt to create a more peaceful atmosphere, I bring Bonnie to stand on the chair by the sink again. She can rinse the plates I have washed. Jack, seeking attention from both the menfolk with the blaring TV and also from us girls in the kitchen, is scampering this way and that. He pokes my leg, slaps my bottom, tugs my shirt as he dodges in and out of the kitchen. "No, thank-you," I sound firm. "Please don't do that," I frown. "Stop it!" my voice is raised. And suddenly I swing my wet hand around to slap his fair little face. Our eyes meet. We are both surprised. I can see the red shape of my hand on his rosy cheek. I have never done such a thing. I never want to again. I cannot take it back. It has been done.

I dry my hands, lift him up. No tears. He has lost the fun on his face. But, he has stopped the rascally romp. If I had invited him to help, he would have been included. Instead I had left him trying to get my attention, this time with such unhappy results.

"Let's get you two into the tub." I step into the bathroom and start the water, strip them down and squeeze some dish soap into the water for foamy bubbles.

Toys, shampoo, pouring, floating... while I go through the necessary scrubbing, they experiment with the bubbles and warm water.

My mind tries to sort out what just happened.

↖↑↗

I have listened to Cheryl tell about her childhood. She is the second oldest of five siblings. They were raised on a real farm with real work. Cheryl was only twelve when her mother died. Much of the domestic and farm work became hers. Her father, Archie, remarried and they all moved from the wide open prairies of Saskatchewan to the fertile Fraser Valley of

British Columbia. Cheryl's step-mother, Fran, had five children of her own. Somehow, Cheryl's leadership and determination orchestrated the houseful of teenagers as they learned to be compatible and strive to make the best of those years before leaving home.

Yes, Cheryl knew a lot about work, but, not so much about play. Married young. Pregnant twice within a year. Cooking for five adults and two children while tending the chickens, goats, garden... her life was still mostly about work.

In comparison, when I was growing up and we lived in Colorado, my Mother was a Sunday School volunteer. In Florida she was a Girl Scout leader. In Ontario she was a kindergarten teacher and foster parent. I observed Mother with small children many times. Fun, learning, obedience, redirecting behaviour, recognizing the abilities of each child's physical development and language skills, these were things I knew about.

Since Cheryl and I have very different background experiences to draw on, our methods of child care are very different.

When Kevin and I had first arrived in Avola, in August, we had been sleeping in our VW van on Fran and Archie's property during the pleasant autumn months before the cabin was finished. I had noticed that whenever I started to engage Cheryl's children by singing those old-fashioned, hand-clapping, finger-plays and well known nursery rhymes, they didn't know the words, actions or songs. I had heard Cheryl scold and shout, but not cuddle and read aloud. She had a rather abrupt bedtime with the children, and only corrected them when they annoyed her by interrupting the quick pace of her work.

↖↑↗

While I rub the towels over Bonnie and Jack's little bodies, I renew my pledge to share what I know with this family. Cheryl

Thursday, March 22, 1979

has already taught me so much about bread dough, pie dough, animals, gardening, canning, jam, pickles, compost and wildlife. I have something valuable to teach her, too.

After Kevin gets a job and the money starts to come in, as soon as we get a vehicle, I want to start a 'Moms and Tots' group. By getting together, the Moms can help each other in practical ways, build up the children's language development, give the little ones opportunities to learn and do art, play and pretend, share and take turns.

Bonnie's pink nightgown, combed hair and furry slippers are a picture. Jack has his red and blue PJs on, teeth brushed. Norman Rockwell should be here to paint them.

The phone rings and I give Cheryl a report of the day. I assure her that everything is running smoothly and they should relax and enjoy their mini-vacation. The children say good-night to their parents.

I try to get the children to say 'good-night' to their uncles without more rowdy teasing. I enjoy arranging the layers of blankets and a cuddly teddy, reading a story book and then "Lights out."

"But, we didn't say our prayers," Bonnie's tiny voice pipes up. "We always say our prayers."

Jack's chin trembles.

I don't want tears and "I miss Mommy! When is Daddy coming home?"

"Tell me how you do it." I hope they can recite their prayers without my prompting. Cheryl didn't tell me about this part of the day. I don't know what to expect. Since the children didn't know much about the Baby Jesus when I came on Christmas Day, I really didn't think there was much evidence of religious instruction in this family.

In unison, these two sweet voices recite:

There are four corners to my bed.
There are four angels at my head.
Matthew, Mark, Luke and John,
bless the bed that I lay on.
Amen.

God bless Mommy and Daddy
and everyone in the whole wide world.
Amen.

"Amen," I reply, with a little hug and a gentle touch to their soft, blond heads.

Finish the dishes. My turn in the tub. Snuggle down with my husband while the TV blares in the next room. Day is done.

I think we will all be OK.

↖↑↗

"We didn't talk about how much you'd like to be paid," Cheryl hesitated to bring up the subject.

"Goodness, Cheryl, you have done so much for Kevin and I. Of course I am glad to volunteer to look after your kids, anytime, for any amount of time. Lifetime privileges!"

However, when she drove us home, a very welcome box of groceries was unloaded.

"Look, Kevin! Jam and pickles, peaches and plums, bread, eggs, potatoes, onions, carrots, turnips, beets. Even a cabbage made it through the winter in her root cellar." I am even more eager for spring to come. Someday I will have this abundance to share from our garden!

Thursday, March 22, 1979

↖↑↗

What Happened Next?

On Tuesday afternoon, March 27, 1979, Kevin was outside, cutting brush to improve our driveway and paths. The snow was melting quickly. The air was softly signalling hope. The Canada geese had returned. The buds on every twig were swelling. The birch trees dangled yellowy-green catkins. Meanwhile, I was puttering about in the cabin with the door wide open.

I heard the motor of a truck stop and a horn sharply break the forest quiet. I heard men's voices.

In a few moments, Kevin returned to the cabin with a grin on his face that I had never seen before.

"Who was it?" I eagerly asked, wishing both to savour the moment and hurry towards what was obviously good news.

"That was the Road Master," he began. I had seen the orange trucks and knew he was talking about the railroad. "He rolled down his window and waved me to come closer. He's a big, round guy. Polish, I'd say from his accent."

"And?" I prompted.

"'Are you the fellow looking to work on the railway?' he asked. 'Yes, that's me." I said. 'Are you a hippy or a farmer?' He looked me up and down. I guess he's had quite a few guys hired and fired because they don't take it seriously to be on time, no drinking on the job, no pot." Kevin liked to tell stories so I could understand and imagine the details. "'I'm a Farmer.' I said. Clearly that made a good impression. 'You got work boots?' he saw the steel toed boots I was wearing. 'Yes, Sir.' I knew I should answer with respect. 'Come to the tool house Monday. We'll see what you can do.' He was rolling up his window to leave. But, since we have no vehicle I had to interrupt. 'I have no truck at the moment.' I explained. 'You stand at the crossing at seven o'clock. Tychkowsky's crew will come and get you. You get first pay. You go buy truck.' And then he turned around and left! I'm in! I have a job!"

Kevin saw my face with an expression he had never seen before. Smiles and tears sometimes go together!

It was the shortest job interview I had ever heard of. But, it was also the beginning of a lifelong career. From now on, we would have stability. From now on, we would have enough to eat.

↖↑↗

"Kevin?" I wonder if he's already sleeping.

"Hmmm?"

"I have music in my head. It's the theme from 'Gone with the Wind.' Da-daaa-da-da" In the tiny cabin in the dark, I sing the melody of the affluent south. "I have never told you, but sometimes this winter, I felt like Scarlett O'Hara when she returns to the plantation, to the destruction, to the poverty after the war. Remember? She stands in the sunset glow and boldly vows, 'If I have to lie, steal, cheat or kill: I will never be hungry again!' We never got to that extreme!" And then, in a heartfelt whisper "Thank God!"

The first part, the cold, dark, alone part, the never-to-be-forgotten part of our 'Back-to-Basics' life was over.

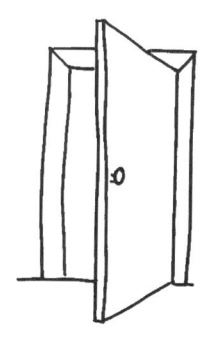

Chapter 2
Friday, February 26, 1982

I learned this at least from my experiment:
That if one advances confidently
in the direction of his dreams,
and endeavours to live the life which he has imagined,
he will meet with success unexpected in common hours.
 —Henry David Thoreau

↘↓↙

At this exact place, in this precise moment, I am exactly where I want to be.

If this was a movie, the warm, rich chords of musical satisfaction would be playing and the credits would signal the end of the drama. The audience would sigh with relief and realize that the young couple and their two small children would indeed 'live happily ever after.'

Still wearing my hospital bracelet, bundled up in my parka, boots stepping out of the truck into the soft, new snow, my eyes drink in the welcome sight. I haven't been home for over a month.

Wait. There is smoke coming out of the chimney. Someone is already here! Mother! She has little Elise in her arms, confused by all of the recent moving and strangers. Kevin is getting the baby out of the car seat in the blue and white Chevy Blazer 4x4. I don't know what is making me more happy? Seeing my little girl again, seeing my Mother again, or seeing my husband carrying his infant son. For the first time, we are a three-generation family in the stackwall house that Kevin built last summer to shelter us all.

Tromping of boots. Shedding of coats. Wrapped in familiar hugs. Smiles and voices, greetings and gestures. We're home.

"How did you get here?" I cannot fathom the fact that my Mother is here... from Florida!

As Mother lowers Elise to the floor, I stoop to make eye contact with her. Elise doesn't like surprises. I pause, reading her face before I claim the hug I so much want to give her.

Kevin passes the baby to Mother. "Meet your first grandson!" he announces with a big grin. He heads back out to the truck to bring in the diaper bag, groceries and refill the wood box. I settle into the rocking chair and bring Elise up onto my lap. Mother is cooing to the baby and enjoying the sensation of holding a newborn.

I look around. Everything is in order. It is February! We are warm! I feel like I have just planted a flag on the top of a mountain after steep terrain, multiple hazards and long endurance.

↘↓↙

1978

Four years ago, this was all a dream. "I want to get married, go out west, build a log cabin, raise a bunch of kids, volunteer in my community and then write a book about it." That was my pledge as a new Bride. And so it was begun.

The summer of 1978, we got married and drove west and found this land. While Kevin built the log cabin, there was very little I could do to help. The logs were simply too heavy. He built it alone. I paid for the lumber for the floor and roof with the wages I earned as a waitress at the Avola Restaurant. I chinked the cracks with moss. I kept the meals coming. But, really, with the cabin, I could only watch and cheer.

1979

Three years ago, married, tucked into our tiny uninsulated log cabin, we endured bitter cold, long winter nights, months of unemployment, meagre meals and crushing isolation. And, yes, I could write a whole book about that part![6]

1980

Two years ago, Kevin's regular pay cheques from the railroad provided for our needs while I was pregnant for the first time. We worked steadily that summer to build this new house, before and after he went to work, before and after our daughter, Elise, was born.

It was great fun building the stackwall house. At first, it was going to be an experiment. "It will be a goat barn," Kevin confidently announced as he began to dig the trench for the cement foundation. "If it works, we'll build a stackwall house later."

"Kevin, those goats will be warmer than we are!" I prompted him to make the experimental building 18x18 feet. With a barn roof for the upstairs, it would be much better living conditions and still satisfy our do-it-yourself, Back-to-the-Land lifestyle.

Building with the stackwall[7] method was much more of a team effort. It was pretty easy for Kevin to dig the footings for the foundation. Since our land was previously a sandbar along an ancient riverbed, the soil was loose gravel, easy to dig. Kevin rigged up 400 feet of black pipe with two gas-powered pumps to bring water up from the river to mix the cement. He filled the pickup truck with sandy grit from a nearby cut along the roadside. He borrowed a gas-powered cement mixer. Every payday, we bought a little more of the supplies we would need. Then, for two weeks, we mixed and poured cement, filling in the foundation with large river-round rocks. Next payday we repeated the process, buy more supplies, prime the pumps, run the water, start the cement mixer, shovel sand, bucket the gloppy muck into place, stand back and admire the progress.

Remembering the Herculean task Kevin had accomplished, cutting the logs for the cabin with an axe and crosscut saw, he was especially glad this time to have a chainsaw! A Jonsereds 801 chainsaw with a 24 inch bar was the first thing Kevin bought with his very first pay cheque. He cut long, thin, dry, jack pine scavenged from the discarded piles he discovered up the logging roads and loaded eight-foot lengths into the pickup truck. While he was working on the railroad, I could do the next two jobs, in-between caring for Baby Elise. Straddling a log, sliding the draw-knife towards me, I peeled off the rough, fragrant bark. Next, I marked one-foot lengths with a thick, yellow crayon.

Since she was born in the summertime, little Elise took her naps in the blue bed I brought outside with mosquito netting tucked securely around her. Later, she sat on a stump in her recliner seat. I was extra-specially careful about how I worked, rolling the logs, cutting with the sharp draw-knife, splitting wood for cooking. I did not want to injure myself and be unable to care for her.

Friday, February 26, 1982

When Kevin revved up the chainsaw to cut the wood into foot-long chunks, I could deliver them into stacks around the four sides of the building site. Over and over again, every payday we bought sacks of dusty grey cement and powdery white lime to make the mortar mix. Yellow rubber gloves were important to protect our hands. One bucket at a time we glopped on the mortar. One block of wood at a time we began to stack the wood onto the foundation. Using a plumb-line, right-angle and level we could guide the walls higher and higher. Each time we went around, we added about three layers of the wooden blocks. There was a pattern to the work, scooping up the muddy mixture in rubber-gloved hands, patting a handful on the inside end of each piece of wood, then the outside edge, leaving a hollow part in-between. When that round was set, we poured grey pellet insulation into the hollow cavity between the inner and outer mortar walls.

Hearing of our project, Heather took the bus from Kananaskis Park in Alberta to come and help with building. Local friends and families interested in the process came to pitch in. Even children could carry the wood, scoop the glop, stack the layers. There was so much to celebrate. Kevin bought a wood cook stove and a wood heater and a generator from a fellow who moved away. He planned out the angles for beams he would need in the shape of a barn roof. Payday. Material. Build. It was all going according to schedule.

But then, in October, when the walls were almost high enough to include the upstairs floor joists, it started to rain. You just can't build with cement in a downpour. We remembered when autumn rains had hampered building on the first cabin. It is to be expected. But this year, there was no return to sunshine. The weather went directly from soggy rain, to frosty cold. You just can't build with cement when it's below freezing. Very disappointed, we realized that circumstances beyond our control would prevent the completion of the stackwall house before winter.

I knew I could not stay in the cabin with Elise, where the indoor temperature would go below freezing.

1981

One year ago, because of the incomplete stackwall house, I decided to take the train to Ontario and spent the winter months with my family in the Arbour Vale Church Community. That was when my parents split up.[8] It was agonizing to be so glad to be with family while so upsetting to try to comprehend the factors involved in their separation.

When I returned on the train to our homestead in April, it wasn't long before a little passenger began to grow inside me, making the building project all the more urgent.

We needed room for two car seats. The blue and white Chevy Blazer replaced the bright green pickup truck.

During the summer months, my brother James and a my best friend's brother, Matthew, came to work for us. The upstairs floor joists were mortared into place and floorboards nailed down. The roof beams lined up. Metal roofing, two skylights, fiberglass insulation, two chimneys and stairs completed the dwelling. The young men left on the train, returning to university in Ontario.

We moved in just before Christmas: husband, wife, toddler, and a big, round belly.

1982

Because I was having contractions often throughout the day and night since my eighth month, Doctor Lam suggested that I not lift Elise or any other loads. Kevin has been handling all

Friday, February 26, 1982

of the firewood, grocery and laundry bags. I got into the habit of sitting before I lifted Elise, holding her on my lap for a story-book, talking, playing with toys or singing.

Although it is called 'false labour,' it was a signal I took seriously. Concerned that I might go into labour while Kevin was away from home, without a phone or radio, no vehicle or neighbours, we asked Fran and Archie if we could stay with them until the birthing day.

A month is a pretty long time to be guests, no matter how patient and generous the hosts are. We paid for our groceries, helped with chores, tried to be quiet and not impose. Last year, Jim and Cheryl and their children had moved into a cute little white house with blue trim in Avola, and the uncles had found a place to live that was closer to the sawmill, so Fran and Archie had moved into the big, old, log farm house. Kevin and Elise and I could sleep in the upstairs where the menfolk used to bunk. We weren't at all crowded.

Still. We weren't exactly being 'Self-Sufficient'!

While we waited for signals that the baby would arrive, I wondered. What would it be like to live out in the wilderness in the middle of winter with two children in diapers?

↘↓↙

And here we are experiencing satisfaction: generous warmth, abundantly fed, steady income, reliable truck, a brand-new house, comfortable marriage, a growing daughter, a brand new son, and a visit from my Mother.

As the poet says,
"God's in His heaven.
All's right with the world."

But, this is not the end of a movie! And so, we begin a new real-life chapter.

↘↓↙

Elise and I are getting reacquainted. She loves to be on my lap. Nursery rhymes and finger-plays have been our main activities this past month. Elise is the prefect age for language development games.

With my Mother looking on and enjoying her granddaughter's clever replies, I begin songs I know that Elise will recognize. "*Do-do-dooo, do-do-dooo, do-do-do-d-doooo*" ... "*Jingle Bells!*" Elise calls out. I start another tune. "*A-B-C-D!*" she knows that one, too. *Partridge in a pear tree, We wish you a merry Christmas, B-I-N-G-O, Eeensy-weensy spider, Twinkle twinkle little star.* The list goes on and on. She is only 20 months old, and does not pronounce every word, but I know that she knows.

Kevin is entertained. Dearma is thrilled. Elise is content. Now I introduce her to her little brother.

"Look, Elise. See Dearma?" This is the name my Mother wants her grandchildren to call her. Not 'Grammie' like I called my father's mother. Not 'Oma' like I called my mother's mother. 'Dearma.'

I signal Kevin to move a chair near me so she can sit down. "Look. Do you see? Who is Dearma holding?"

"Baby," Elise answers. She has seen other babies at the 'Moms and Tots' group in Avola.

"Yes. Look at his tiny fingers. Touch his soft head. This is your brother, Michael. Can you say 'Michael'? He is in our family now. Would you like to hold him?" Still sitting on my lap, firmly holding them both, Dearma helps me make the introductions. "Michael, this is your sister, Elise."

Friday, February 26, 1982

Kevin snaps the camera. Elise is grinning. Michael is still asleep. Dearma is where she has always wanted to be. My heart is overflowing.

↘↓↙

After the birth, Doctor Lam warned that I should not lift anything heavier than ten pounds for another month. So, Dearma and Kevin are looking after my needs. Water buckets, diaper bags, firewood, compost buckets, carrying Baby Michael up the stairs, lifting Elise in and out of the truck. My jobs are sleep and rest, eat and drink, sing to Elise, and nurse Michael.

Dearma is familiar with much of our philosophy and purpose. She came to visit us in the cabin during the summer of 1979, after that first winter. I went to stay with her last winter.

Before we were married, Kevin and I decided to enter the 'Back-to-the-Land' lifestyle. We wanted to heat with wood, drink water from a mountain creek, grow our own food, bring up our children surrounded by Nature, learn practical skills, and live a simple life on one income. Now, when we have problems to solve, we have a variety of skills and resources. Do-it-yourself and bartering are a part of our economy.

With two children in diapers, the trend is to use disposable diapers. But, no. I decided not to do that when I was seventeen years old! While I was babysitting for a family with twin baby boys, I watched the mom arrive home from shopping with a huge case of diapers every week. I mentally did the math. Those two tiny boys would fill an entire garage with non-biodegradable waste before they were toilet trained!

Since we live without electricity or running water, we have asked a neighbour in Avola if Kevin can come in and do a load of laundry every couple of days. We have about 70 diapers in rotation!

February Chapter 2

Living 45 miles from a store, we have stocked up on supplies and filled the pantry, anticipating winter roads and infrequent trips to Clearwater. Happily, my body is generously supplying milk to this baby as I did for the first one. No refrigeration needed. But, boy, do I have to eat and drink a lot! I have been pregnant and nursing for sixteen months and, without a break in-between, I probably have another sixteen months to go.

↘↓↙

The stackwall house is such an improvement over the 14x14 foot log cabin with the sleeping loft that we built the first year. Now we have 18x18 foot downstairs, plus a full upstairs with a barn roof. South facing, the big windows and skylights let in lots of natural light, even on overcast days. The cement foundation supports the thick, insulated walls and closes in the crawl space so no frigid air is getting sucked in through the cracks in the floorboards, like there was in the original log cabin. We have two wood stoves now which is another major improvement to our living situation. The white enamel cook stove has a warming oven, hot water reservoir and an accurate oven thermometer. On the far side of the dwelling, the wood heater holds enough wood to last all night. We can sleep! We have a full woodshed! The insulated upstairs sleeping area is toasty warm! Yes, having a warm and cozy place for a newborn baby in February is a real accomplishment.

Kevin will be going back to work after this first family day together. He is the night patrolman on the railroad. He leaves the house at 10:00pm to drive up to Avola. Every night he talks to the Dispatcher in Kamloops on the telephone to get the Line-Up at exactly 11:00pm. The Line-Up lists when each train is leaving the cities to the north and south. Kevin has to calculate the speed and distance to know when each train is expected to pass through and when he had better be off the tracks. Then he loads his lunch, a head lamp, kerosene lamp and emergency flares onto a three-wheeled bike. Because both passenger trains, east-bound and west-bound, will pass through several rock cuts during the night, he pedals out on the train tracks to visually inspect the track before they arrive. The engineers contact him by radio before they proceed through the river-carved canyon. After he pedals the nine miles back to Avola, he gets off work at 7:00am and returns home to sleep.

Dearma will need to know how to operate the cook stove, add wood to the heater, and light the kerosene lamp. Upstairs, we have set up mattresses on the floor to make a huge double-double bed. Kevin will sleep in the daytime. I will come and go with nursing and to lie down with Elise for an afternoon nap. Dearma will come to sleep after Kevin leaves for work. A 'family bed' seems the best option for us to look after the needs of the children during the night, especially since my husband is far away. We all keep warm and secure.

↘↓↙

While I nurse the baby, and Elise is content with her toys, Kevin takes Dearma on the Grand Tour.

"You can see right here, how we built the walls this high before we had to stop when it started to rain," he explains. "See how the lumber for the upstairs floor joists were mortared into place. The beams for the barn roof were sheathed with metal roofing, then we insulated the roof, so it is much better than the cabin. After I stapled clear plastic over the pink fiberglass insulation, then Eleanor stapled up these sheets of fabric. She likes the colours."

Dearma moved to Florida after she and Daddy separated. I am so glad she came to help out. She travelled the day

Michael was born, but it takes two days to get here. One day to fly to Edmonton, then another day on the Greyhound to get to Avola. She stayed with Fran and Archie, getting to know Elise (who was staying with Cheryl), and waited for me to return home.

"I brought home milk yesterday," Kevin prompts me to get back to a regular routine. "We get one of these gallon glass jars full of fresh milk every three days," he explains to Dearma.

"See how the cream rises?" I interrupt. "I usually skim it off. I have been trying to make butter, but so far I only shake it long enough to make whipped cream!" Dearma looks surprised. She is slim and trim and doesn't really want to participate in eating whipped cream every three days! "I think that's why Michael grew so big! Whenever I got hungry I would have milk and bran muffins. This entire baby is made out of milk and bran muffins... and whipped cream! Did I tell you? He was nine pounds, eleven ounces!" Remembering the effort, I gaze at my 'little' baby.

"I thought he looked and felt pretty big," Dearma comes over to admire him again.

"When they put the newborn nightie on him, he stretched out his arm and the sleeve only came half way between his elbow and his wrist," I explain. "And the newborn diaper barely made it around his middle. He weighs the same as some babies who are three months old!"

"So, if the doctor said not to carry anything over ten pounds you can't even lift your own baby!" she exclaims.

"Oh, right! I hadn't thought of that," I shake my head and look again at this big little man. "I have been adding the cream to our porridge, topping every soup, and spreading whipped cream on peanut butter sandwiches. I suppose it will come in handy for me to have this many extra calories while I am nursing him," I add. "In fact, I could use a snack right now."

Friday, February 26, 1982

"I think I should bring you food and something to drink every time you nurse him," Dearma is ready for her duties.

"Before you do, please let me give you this present," I nod to Kevin to reach the wrapped gift we have prepared for this occasion.

It is a burgundy coloured t-shirt with white letters, custom made for the new Grandmother. "Dearma Fan Club!" she reads the inscription. "And, what's this?" There is a little white flannel nighty. I wrote on it in red permanent marker, 'Dearma Fan Club' for baby Michael to wear.

The dog barking signals that a truck is coming up the driveway. Kevin goes to the door. "Cheryl's here! And the children, too."

Greetings are exchanged. The baby is admired. Kevin supervises the children outside in the snow so we can have some girl-time.

"Adele phoned. I told her I'd come down to visit you right away so I could give her an accurate report." Cheryl covers her own curiosity with the responsibility of communicating over the phone with Kevin's Mom. "Look at the size of him!" she exclaims as she hoists the lad, holding him in her confident and experienced way, covering his face with smooches.

"I used the pay-phone at the hospital to let her know the news," I recall. "I'm sure she'd like to have up-dates daily like she had while we were staying at Fran and Archie's place."

Turning to my Mother, I relate a story that Cheryl already knows. "The day before I went into labour, Kevin had gone to Kamloops. I had been feeling very droopy, tired, useless, sleeping all the time, heavy and awkward with this enormous belly. Kevin brought me a book." Lynne Johnston, Canadian creator of the daily newspaper cartoon strip, 'For Better or Worse,' had recently published 'David! We're Pregnant!' which is a book of one page drawings for the expectant couple. "It sure made me laugh."

"While I read each page, following various couples from before pregnancy, through all of the hormonal and physical changes, the emotions of delivery and celebrating the 'bundle of joy,' I started to cry. My husband, thinking I didn't like it, looked upset. But, it was his tender kindness that was making me cry. 'Do you love me?' I sobbed, looking up at him through foggy tears. He looked bewildered. 'Of course,' was his reply." I continue my story.

"I said, 'But, today is *your* birthday, and I didn't prepare *anything* for you. And here you are giving me a present,' I just couldn't comprehend it at all. 'Fran made you a dinner and a birthday cake. All I did today was sleep.' I felt really miserable." Sometimes emotions are hard to comprehend.

"My husband was so kind. 'That's your job right now. You are the one making the biggest present of all. There would be no baby if not for the work you are doing,' he reassured me." Making eye contact with Kevin is like vitamins for me.

"'Oh,' I sobbed. 'I didn't think of it that way.'" Silly me!

"To comfort me, after supper Fran offered to put my hair in curlers. In the middle of the night, when I realized that labour had begun, I quickly took the rollers out, ran a comb through my hair and woke up Kevin to take me to the hospital in Clearwater. And that is how I arrived at the hospital looking like Raggedy-Anne." It is strange how it all happened only four days ago.

"Later, Cheryl joined us, and it was a good thing to have an experienced mother with me through the changes and effort of the day." Cheryl and I share a hug.

"We are both doing very well. Thanks for coming, Cheryl. And thanks for coaching me through labour. I have to admit, the first time, when Elise was born, I was all 'skipping through the daisies.' I thought that a cheerful attitude, and cooperating with the forces of Nature, and being thankful to God would keep me immune to the troubles some women experience. Now I know that it takes a long time and focused concentration. There's only so much you can learn through books and asking your friends what it is like. There are some parts of the process that are very hard work. This time I went to prenatal classes and I knew what labour was like from experience. But still, I was a little anxious to repeat the endurance test that giving birth really is," I confide in the two women.

I meet Cheryl's eyes. I have a foggy memory of struggling, confused by the strength of Nature's forces, whining and wishing there was such a thing as taking a break from the hours of pressure and demanding sensations.

"I remember that I got a little panicky and kind of dizzy. I just kept thinking, 'I wish I was someplace else... If I could just have ten minutes to rest!' But, there is no turning back once you get started. Your voice came to me, clear and steady and certain, 'Eleanor, use your breath to push!' That really helped me a lot." Cheryl's command had cut through the confusion, right when I wanted to give up. And, sure enough, Michael was born.

"Look at the size of him!" Cheryl is opening his wraps and examining his features. "My first baby was around six pounds! Michael is a giant!"

Women gain strength from each other while telling and listening to birthing stories. Now I have stories, too.

↘↓↙

What Happened Next?
Michael was full to overflowing with physical strength and energy. I got tired just watching him when he was a baby and toddler. Elise gained language early and was so cooperative.

Michael spoke much later. His frustration and mine, combined with his curiosity and determination, brought us to many moments of conflict. But, no matter where we were along the Path of Life, birthdays were always a fun event.

First Birthday: Michael took his first steps just as I clicked the camera!

Two years old: The neighborhood children came and we made a train with boxes, pretending to take a trip to the zoo, ocean, city and mountaintop.

Three years old: 'M' shaped cake. Half of the letter was made with an angel food cake. The other half was made with a devil's food cake.

Four years old: Kevin's Mom sent a Garfield cake pan! It was tricky to make and I needed a lot of toothpicks to hold it together. The birthday guests used blocks and all kinds of toys and filled the living room floor with a town including a museum, airport, farm and zoo.

Five years old: Grampa Hinkle sent a Lego spaceship kit. Dad and Lad worked on it together, but when Michael started to shoot the inhabitants of other planets, Kevin intervened, "No matter where we go and no matter who we discover living there, the same God who made us, made these people, also. So there will be no weapons. You may explore and learn. You may not kill."

Six years old: Grampa Hinkle sent a pirate flag! I made an island cake with a walnut shell pirate ship and a treasure hunt with all of the birthday gifts as the prize.

Seven years old: The party had a Cowboy theme with little toy buffalo and horses galloping across the cake.

Eight years old: Michael invited a guest to sleep over and we each made a do-it-yourself pizza.

Nine years old: "Can we watch movies for nine hours? Can we have nine treats?" Michael requested.

Friday, February 26, 1982

Ten years old: Inspired by the giant spiders' webs in 'The Hobbit,' Michael and his guest claimed the whole living room, lacing string into an impenetrable web-maze.
… and many more...

Chapter 2
Tuesday, March 9, 1982

> I am only one, but I am one.
> I cannot do everything, but I can do something.
> And I will not let what I cannot do
> interfere with what I can do.
> —Edward Everett Hale

↖↑↗

Kevin has been working all night. The railroad requires a night patrolmen through the rock-cuts before the passenger trains come through the canyon. He leaves the house at 10:00pm, works 11:00pm-7:00am, and is home about 20 minutes later. He goes straight to bed while I get the children dressed, nursed, fed. Dearma helps choreograph the morning so that everyone's needs are met.

It's Tuesday, my favourite day of the week. The 'Moms and Tots' group gets together from 10:30 until noon. Today I will introduce both my Mother and my newborn son.

At about 10:00am, I gently rouse Kevin. He is quick to be ready to drive us all back to Avola. While he goes to the post office and meets the men who are maintaining machinery at the workshop, we ladies have a little morning outing with our preschoolers, tots and infants.

While we drive along the highway, I explain the situation to my Mother. She has also run a volunteer preschool, when my youngest sister, Carol, was a toddler. Later, she taught kindergarten and then the three primary grades. So I have gleaned ideas from her example.

"The very first autumn when we arrived, Cheryl's daughter, Bonnie, had her first day of kindergarten. She was so shy, Cheryl thought she might cling and cry and have a very emotional first day. I offered to take her. Although Bonnie was somewhat withdrawn, she also had a fun time and was able to go to school by herself after that." It's fun to remember that day.

"The next autumn, I asked if I could volunteer at the school," I continue. "There are only two classrooms for all eight grades plus kindergarten. It was so enjoyable to participate. Now that I have my own children, it seems like a good time to start a 'Moms and Tots' playgroup. We meet at the Community Hall."

↖↑↗

The Community Hall in Avola was built in 1937 by the Finn brothers. Their skill at log building was also put to work to build the one room log schoolhouse and teacher's little log house up the hill. A plain, open room with windows along both sides, the Community Hall has been in continuous use for movie nights (the train brought reels of film from the library), youth floor hockey (supervised by adults), dances (getting a liquor licence was easy to do), town meetings (with separate volunteer committees looking after the cemetery, water system, parks and recreation), and the annual school Christmas Concert (when every resident came to see the children recite, sing, act and anticipate a visit from Santa). A voting booth was set up for elections. Weddings and funerals, baby showers and good-bye parties have all been held here. With an outhouse in the back, a propane furnace and cook stove, tables along the walls and chairs stacked and ready for the next event, all that is needed is some Community Spirit and anything can happen here.

Volunteers take care of cleaning, maintenance and improvements. Funding is provided by grants from the lotteries, local donations and fundraisers. It is a system that benefits everyone.

Today, the Community Hall will benefit the babies, toddlers, preschoolers and mothers in our town. The young mothers gather after their morning chores are done, while the older children are in school. They can interact, encourage each other, share experiences and build a web of connections.

ᚲ↑ᚱ

Cheryl has the key to the Community Hall. She gets there first because she knows how to get the furnace started. The pilot light has to be lit every week. Rolling up a newspaper, she lights the tip. Down on her knees, she reaches way back into and underneath the machinery. Whoosh! The flames flicker orange and blue.

While the building warms up, she walks across the street to the post office.

Mrs. Buis is the Post Mistress. With 250 residents and several businesses, she has a lot of mail to sort into the boxes. People can buy stamps and money orders, weigh parcels, fill out Customs forms and send and receive registered mail. But most importantly, people often stay to chat and exchange local news, such as illness and guests, highway conditions and cute kids. 'Who's going to town today?' and 'Can you bring back a few items?' Even our new baby and my Mother coming to visit have been discussed.

The post office is a small lobby with 100 brass mailboxes. The lobby is open from 8:00am-8:00pm. Mrs. Buis comes in at about 10:00 when the mail truck bringing deliveries from Kamloops is expected. It takes until about 10:30 for Mrs. Buis to sort the mail in a locked room. When it is ready, she opens the window for business.

Visiting with neighbours is a highlight of the day. Parents make a point of walking to the post office at 10:30 while the children are outside for recess. The school children and the town residents are closely connected.

↖↑↗

The first school in Avola was a frame building south of town. After the forest fires of 1929 destroyed the settlement further downriver, the building was dragged up on the river ice by a sturdy team of horses.

The same Finn Brothers who built the log Community Hall were hired to build the more permanent one room log Avola Schoolhouse in 1939. The logs were harvested from nearby. The forest fires had left dead cedar trees standing. The timber was exceptionally well preserved when the sap boiled within the trees as the fires swept the forest floor. This historic building has been used as the school gym since the early 1970s when the present three room school was constructed from portable classroom units.

Twenty-six children study their lessons in two of the classrooms. The third room is multi-purpose. Mrs. Olson teaches Grades 1-3 and also kindergarten in the morning three days

Tuesday, March 9, 1982

a week. Mr. Archer has Grades 5-8. There are no Grade 4 students this year.

When the teacher rings the brass bell at 9:00, all 26 children line up at the door. After the teacher calls each name for attendance, the children stand, bow their heads and recite the Lord's Prayer. When they are seated again, one of the older children reads aloud a short passage from the Bible. Then everyone stands again to sing, *O Canada*. The rotation of subjects follows so that the teacher can pay attention to individuals in each age group while the others are doing seat work with little supervision. Reading, writing, spelling and math all have textbooks for each grade. Social studies, science, art, PE and music can be taught to the whole group. One teacher with about a dozen children; it looks ideal to me.

Outdoors, during good weather, the teachers help the children modify team sports to best include every age. Baseball, soccer, hockey, as well as variations of tag, jump rope rhymes and bounce ball games are part of the rural physical education program. On rainy days and through the winter, the log schoolhouse is used as a gym for floor hockey, volley ball, relay races and fitness exercises. The children also have active recess activities on the swings, slide, monkey bars and they play games on the paved area.

Volunteers are welcome. Parents sign up to prepare the hot lunch on Fridays as a fundraiser for field trips planned to the city in the springtime. Moms bring refreshments for special days. The whole town generously supports additional school fundraisers such as selling chocolate bars or wrapping paper, pledging for a walk-a-thon or the annual 'World Hunger Day' 24-hour fast. Other donations pay for fireworks and hot dogs for Halloween. The ladies club arranges the Christmas gift exchange and candy bags for Santa to give each child.

Within the cycle of the year, school routines are punctuated with holidays. New Years Eve, Valentines Day, Easter, Mother's Day, Father's Day, Canada Day, Thanksgiving, Halloween, Christmas. Each holiday has art projects, songs, poems to recite, decorations to make, perhaps a link to geography or history, new vocabulary, perhaps pretend or costume play for the younger children.

Within the cycle of the month, the older students produce a town newspaper using the ditto machine to run off the purple ink copies on long foolscap paper. 'Tiny Timber News' includes interviews, jokes, upcoming events, news, history, recipes, advertisements and drawings.

Within the cycle of the day, these two teachers bring knowledge of the outside world to these mountain children. The railroad first took passengers in 1916. The highway was paved in 1969. Television and electricity was installed in 1973. The school teachers have a big responsibility to prepare these students for a wider world.

Yes, the school is the hub of the whole town.

↖↑↗

In 1979, when Kevin's pay cheques started coming in, he bought a pickup truck. At first, Kevin was working in the daytime, so I could get a ride with him early in the morning before his 7:00am shift started. He dropped me off at Cheryl's house. I played with the children so Cheryl could sleep in. Then we did chores together and she taught me so many practical things. When it was time, we headed down to Avola.

I wanted to volunteer at the school because I enjoy it so much, but also to develop trust with the children and the parents and get to know the people. Once a week, I came to the school for a whole day, all through my first pregnancy. In

Tuesday, March 9, 1982

the Primary room, I read aloud and played with dice to practice adding and times tables. Mrs. Olson often ended the day with a game, "Heads down, thumbs up, let's play 7-up!" In the Intermediate room, I taught the girls to cook pancakes, omelettes and spaghetti. I also liked to bring my guitar and expand the children's musical repertoire.

Elise was born in the summer of 1980, so when September brought the children back-to-school, I wanted to volunteer again. However, because our cabin was too cold, baby Elise and I returned to Ontario for the winter months. When I returned, Kevin and I had to focus on finishing our building project. I became pregnant again. Elise was a toddler. I decided the time was right to start the 'Moms and Tots' playgroup so I could teach the women what I know about: small children.

↖↑↗

Kevin unbuckles baby Michael and passes him to Dearma. Then he carries Elise into the Hall. I bring the red diaper bag. Kevin comes back for a big box filled with storybooks, balls, bean bags, a simple craft project and a cardboard game I made.

Here they come!

Cheryl's here with her son, Mason. She was newly pregnant when we first arrived and now he's nearly three years old. Bonnie and Jack are both in school now. Her husband and mine work on the train tracks. The worse the weather, the more they are needed. Cheryl unwraps Mason's scarf, but leaves his boots and coat on. The floor is still cold. With her is the school teacher's son, Karl. He will be in kindergarten next year. Tall, blond and shy, he is an only child and his Dad looks after him while his Mom is at school. It is fun to see how he interacts with the others.

Noisy and rambunctious, brothers Charlie and Nate hurry to the box of blocks and balls. They like to set up a bowling alley and soon all the boys are knocking down obstacles with a clatter, laughter and cheering. Their Dad also works on the railroad and they live near the train tracks. Their Mom, Opal, regularly takes them to Sunday School in Blue River where they have relatives.

Always smiling, Debbie arrives with her energetic older son and shy little daughter. Her older daughter is in school, and her husband is a mechanic who works on the logging trucks and road building equipment. Debbie has a box of crackers, a block of cheese, a bag of apples and a jug of juice. By taking turns providing refreshments, we have avoided any kind of fee for this group.

With them is a neighbour child. His mother and grandparents run the Log Inn Pub. He can't always come. Running a small business means frequent long days to go to the city for supplies. But, he knows the other boys and they continue their bowling game while the mothers greet each other and get settled.

I introduce my Mother, everyone passes little Michael around. Elise stays close to me. She is not used to all the activity, noise and the echoing, big room.

We have a routine and so we begin.

Good morning to you,
good morning to you,
good morning to Mason,
good morning to all.

One by one, each smiling child is named. This leads the transition from free play to organized activities.

Tuesday, March 9, 1982

As the mothers sing, they guide their children to come up the ramp to the smaller, warmer room and sit together in a circle. Moms and Tots now follow along while we sing nursery rhymes. Little ones are wide-eyed. The older ones know all the words. 'Face-to-face' play stimulates language development. The child learns to read facial expressions and builds trust and bonding. Parenting is a huge undertaking. Many situations come up in a day. Relaxed, structured play gives small children positive examples of the benefit of obedience and following the parents' leadership. The children see each other cooperating and get practice which will improve routines at home. The parents have an example of how to guide children through the day without resorting to scolding, bribes, and other less effective measures.

We move from seated songs to standing in a circle. *Here We Go 'Round the Mulberry Bush* has actions demonstrating washing the dishes, sweeping the floor, brushing your hair, and other domestic daily activities. *The Farmer in the Dell* gives everyone a way to take turns. *Hokey Pokey* is silly and fun and is usually what we end with.

Now it is story time. Either one mother reads to everyone, or else, each family chooses a book and spends a moment reading aloud or talking about the pictures.

Snack time is next. We move from the warmer, smaller room to the large kitchen. Oops! A drink is spilled. I see it instantly turn to ice on the linoleum floor.

Running in the big open room with rolling balls, playing tag and learning to play active games in this open space is good for expending some energy. The long winter months restrict how small children can play, so allowing big physical play is very important. *Red Light – Green Light* and *Mother May I?* are old fashioned games that the children like. Sometimes we pretend. "Who can gallop like a pony? Waddle like a duck? Hop like a bunny? Fly like an eagle?" These questions keep the children together, moving, but not scattered and reduces the risk of mishaps. Bean bags don't roll away. Big boxes become a train. *Follow-the-Leader* brings everyone up onto the stage, down the steps, behind, under and in-between the chairs and tables. Twirling, jumping, hopping, side-stepping all improve large motor skills.

After a romp, we return to the smaller, warmer room. The craft has to be simple enough to complete in a few minutes, satisfying for little hands, but of interest to the older children, too.

Matching, tracing, folding, cutting, painting can be introduced to small children with adult supervision. Play-dough, sock puppets, dress-up clothes or hats encourage pretend and role-play. These activities stimulate ideas we explore together here, which might also stimulate creativity at home.

Today I have brought a cardboard game I made during that last month before the baby was born. Each parent-child pair has a long piece of cardboard on which I have glued a row of large colourful shapes. In addition, there are small colourful shapes cut out for the children to use one-by-one. I demonstrate. "Elise, can you put the small red circle on the large red circle? Can you put the small yellow triangle on the large green square?" Quiet concentration unifies each group while they continue to focus on the task.

And then, our time is up.

Helping hands, helping hands,
my hands will be helping hands,
hang up clothes, pick up toys
help the other girls and boys...

Tuesday, March 9, 1982

We sing together, the parents demonstrating and guiding their children to clean up. And then the good-bye song.

*The more we get together,
together, together,
the more we get together,
the happier we'll be.*

Zip up coats. Turn off the furnace. "See you next time."

↖↑↗

To make the most of her trip from the farm into Avola today, Cheryl brought eggs from her chickens to take to regular customers. She also keeps in touch with the elderly. Tea time and friendship with the seniors brings stories of humour, wisdom and sometimes extreme experiences. One lady, years ago, kept her premature baby warm in a box on the open wood stove oven door.

Cheryl is going to Clearwater tomorrow. There isn't a grocery store in Avola. The gas station sells pop, chips and candy. Under the Log Inn Pub there is a one room store with canned goods on the shelves so the bachelors can grab something for supper. Families usually do their shopping 45 miles away in Clearwater. Cheryl, like the other women, carefully plans a long and detailed list anticipating meals, birthdays and stocking up on sale items. It is important to keep enough baking supplies, and the pantry shelves and freezer full to avoid running out of necessities when the highway is impassable during the winter snows. Cheryl often does grocery shopping for Barb Liscumb, a shut-in lady who lives nearby.

In a small town, there are many interconnections which keep everyone safe and provided for.

While we were romping, learning and playing, Kevin has been to the post office for news and the mail. He also filled two five-gallon water jugs to bring home. Next, he stopped in at the mechanical shop where the menfolk swap stories in-between welding, oil changes and checking the hydraulics. Most have relocated again and again to follow the logging opportunities: road building, felling, bucking, loading, or driving truck to the sawmill. A few have generational ties to the valley. Several men have horses. One raises rabbits. One fellow has established a large aviary, raising prize budgies, doves, finches and a large white cockatoo.

As we pull up the hill, out of town, we pass tiny company houses, mobile homes, original log homesteader's cabins, and structures built by owners before building codes came into effect. The snow covers lawns, vegetable gardens and the Buis' lovely flowerbeds which will overflow with tulips and daffodils, lilacs and lupines when spring returns. The snow hides backyard rubble, piles of firewood and abandoned vehicles.

The gas station and restaurant look busy. Locals drive up on their snowmobiles or 4x4 pickup trucks to meet for coffee. Loggers take a break after their risky ride off the mountain. Tourists and delivery truck drivers know the restaurant is open 24-hours, seven days a week. Long-haul truck drivers pull over to sleep since Avola is the mid-point between Edmonton and Vancouver.

Up to speed on the highway, I can see that winter's white still cloaks the wilderness.

Migratory birds and fish will be returning soon. Hibernating bears will seek the valley bottom as spring unfolds nutritious greenery. First Nations People's wintered in sunny Kamloops and only came upriver in the summer months. There are networks of trails and pathways like threads weaving through these forests.

Explorers, trappers and prospectors made use of the river and old trails. Settlers arrived in the early 1860s. Surveyors mapped the railroad. Since 1916, twice each week, in both directions, trains carried passengers and cargo to local stops. Not so long ago, the rutty dirt road was often hazardous or impassable. Each little village depended on the railroad to bring needed supplies and take residents to the city for medical treatments. Most recently, the oil pipeline (1952), paved highway (1969) and electric power lines (1973) became ribbons of connection along the valley bottom. Each little village had to be self-sufficient.

The new highway transformed the limitations and opened up possibilities. The first wave of homesteaders had come and gone. Now, many abandoned homesteads are easy to see from the highway and along the logging roads. Our property is one of them. I wonder whether many more 'Back-to-the-Land' people will come to this beautiful place and re-populate the valley?

Off the highway, along our narrow road, branches hanging heavy with snow, up to our cozy little home. We return to our own routines and customs, naps and meals, diapers and songs. We are a family!

↖↑↗

What Happened Next?
Dearma went back to Florida.

Elise continued to delight us with her clever learning, questions and entertaining participation in our family life.

Michael grew strong and healthy.

Kevin faced many challenges on the railroad.

I managed this expanding family, preparing bread and meals, keeping the fire, budgeting daily water, bringing new experiences to our children, continuing to volunteer one day per week in the community of Avola.

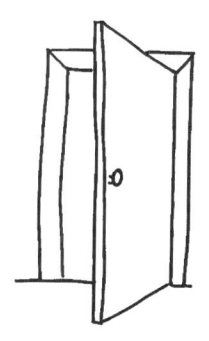

Chapter 3
Wednesday, February 1, 1984

> Do what you can
> with what you have
> where you are.
> —*Theodore Roosevelt*

↘↓↙

It is still winter. February the first. For me, February is the longest month of the year.

The monotony is hard to take. I feel so discouraged. Yes, of course I made New Year's Resolutions. But, how can I improve my fitness when it is so slippery outside? How can I get to know more people and have fun when I have to cancel outings because of illness or weather? How can I enjoy music or begin a new craft project when I just want to curl up in a blanket?

Is there anything to look forward to?

What can I do? ... Today?

February Chapter 3

This is my fifth winter since we got married, and my first winter living in our four-room house in the town of Avola.

Kevin is still working all night and sleeping for part of the day. When he gets up at midday, he goes out to shovel snow, help the elderly clear their roofs and driveways, chats with the men, repairs machinery. Then he eats supper and goes back to sleep. He gets up to leave for work after I have put the children to bed. We are hardly ever in the same place at the same time.

Elise is three-and-a-half, eager to learn, wanting new experiences. I love to read books with her, play pretend and encourage her to do many things for herself. She can get dressed, put on her boots, brush her teeth, clean off her place at the table. She likes to stand on the bench beside my work counter and help me in the kitchen. She's a chatterbox. I feel like I have a buddy. Whatever we do together feels satisfying.

Michael is turning two in a few days. I have heard of 'the terrible twos,' but Elise spared me the struggle. She was cooperative and could speak enough for me to understand when she wanted or didn't want something. Michael is a challenge at every turn. He hardly talks. Instead he fusses and kicks if he doesn't get what he wants. I guess, and offer, and try, but it seems I cannot understand. This only infuriates him further. He is so quickly stubborn when I say, "No." I feel like I am wrestling. I feel like I have to outwit him as we move from sleep to getting dressed, through breakfast and into snowsuits, to come when I call him and lay down for a nap. I have never felt so frustrated while caring for a small child before. How can something I am so good at and that I love so much become such an unpleasant ongoing battle?

Cheryl says, "three spanks" and he is wearing a double thick diaper, so I know I am not actually hurting him, but still, I have never spanked anyone! I am mad at myself every day.

I have no one to confide in, or be coached by, or hand the kids to so I can have a break.

Wednesday, February 1, 1984

↘↓↙

I thought my dreary midwinter slump would not happen this year. We left our homestead out in the woods and moved into Avola last September. Now we live in a little four-room house which was built by dragging three sheds together. The rain drips in where the sheets of metal roofing meet up, and where previous residents have chopped at the ice which forms on the roof because the insulation is so thin.

The long living room features a big window looking out at the street, a wood stove, couch, desk with a dial telephone and always scattered toys. A single light bulb on the ceiling of each room is a big improvement over the kerosene lamp we used in the stackwall house and cabin. The cedar chest Kevin built for me in the cabin was a good place to set up a small Christmas tree for the first time.

Both the front door and the back entry way come straight into the little kitchen and dining area. The wood cook stove and propane hot water tank generate warmth to dry the laundry hanging up high on strings. The work counter Kevin built for me in the stackwall house is within reach of the white refrigerator and green propane stove, very handy for me to prepare our food. Up against the work counter is a bench the children stand on. While I chop and stir they sample tasty bits. The table, chairs and dish cupboard are crowded by the yellow washing machine that shares plumbing with the kitchen sink. The woodshed is out the back door. I have to sweep up bits of bark every day.

We still share one bedroom. I like to be near the children while Kevin is away at night. Kevin has set up the other small room with his tools and projects. The tiny bathroom has a pink bathtub, sink and toilet. Pink is not my favourite colour. However, running water is the best part of living here.

There is nothing actually 'wrong' with my life. That's part of what makes it feel so bad! I do not have any serious problems. Why do I feel so glum?

I have tried a few alternatives to help myself stay out of the dreary doldrums.

Colour helps. Drawing, sewing, even library books filled with photos are like vitamins. When my eyes are happy, I can feel my heart lift. Quilting is my favourite. Laying colourful pieces of fabric side-by-side is very enjoyable. Not only the colours, but the memories of each scrap remind me of my family. Here are blue and gold tiny flowers Mother used for a Thanksgiving tablecloth. Here is a pink spray of flowers she made into an Easter dress for my younger sister, Julie. Here is a handsome plaid of royal blue and grey which was a shirt for my brother, James. I used this dark green to make a skirt for myself back in high school.

Another highly valued benefit of working on quilts is the satisfaction of making something that will last. Every other part of my day is spent, and in the end there is nothing left to show for it.

Clean diapers get poopy. The cat and dog's dishes are filled, then empty. Clean dishes become sticky and stay stacked beside the sink. The compost bucket never seems to be emptied. Like the garbage can and laundry basket, it overflows.

I talked to my Mother on the telephone recently and I told her, "One day I heard the laundry pile laughing at me!"

'A woman's work is never done.' I thought that was a charming saying when I was a bride. I would be like Cinderella and Snow White. I saw myself working steadily, but humming all the while. I would have a charming cottage and trustworthy husband, healthy children and pleasant duties filling my days and challenging my creativity to provide for my home.

Wednesday, February 1, 1984

Now that the dream has become a reality, what can I do to shift my attitude? This endless cycle of repetitive chores is pressing me down. How can I shift from feeling stuck in the limitations and reach towards the possibilities?

Music helps. Daddy sent us Christmas money again this year and we found a record player, amplifier and speakers in the Sears catalogue. Kevin's Mom sent records from the Thrift Store near her home. We also have a cassette deck and the children and I like Raffi. *Baby Beluga* is certainly a cheerful tune. We have a small black and white TV too. 'The Friendly Giant,' 'Curious George,' 'Mr. Dress-Up' and 'Sesame Street' give me two hours every day to spend on my own interests while the children are sitting still.

Although I feel so weary, maybe I should address my physical fitness? Bringing in firewood, bending and lifting to hang up laundry on the string above the stove, even taking the children outside gives me some physical activity. But, I never have the space or time to move as I choose, dance, stretch, do exercises, play a sport.

Cheryl says she wants to start a ladies fitness class on Tuesdays while the Community Hall furnace is still heating the room, after the 'Moms and Tots.' But, who will look after my children while I do that? If I do one sit up, then have to run after a naughty son or have to go look for my daughter, what is the good of that? Besides, I am so fat. 136 pounds! Yuck! I hate the way I look. I only wear baggy, loose clothes so no one can see my shape. If I wear tight clothes to exercise, I will die of embarrassment.

I feel mad at myself every single day. Nothing I plan ever gets finished. Nothing I want is available. Nothing is happening the way I imagined it. I run all day and never get anywhere. This is not how I imagined my life would be.

We have a subscription to the newspaper now. There are photos of club activities, announcements of upcoming events, groups doing worthwhile projects. But, they are all far away in Clearwater. I don't have a driver's license and Kevin has to sleep every day. It takes too much money to pay for gas to go to Clearwater just for fun. We only go once every two weeks for payday. I am stuck here. If I could be with people, I know I would be more cheerful. Knowing that I cannot participate just pulls me further down.

Inside, silently, although I would never admit it, I am moaning! Winter seems soooo long!

Sometimes I just wish I was someplace else!

So, I try to look for tiny things, daily things, some fragment of a thing that will occupy my mind, buoy my spirits, bring me cheer, make me feel like my time on the planet is worthwhile.

Today, I have to knead bread, while watching the clock. My husband wants me to wake him in time for lunch. Repeating the rhythmic push-fold-press-turn with my hands on the bread dough, I suddenly have a surge of realization.

My love for my husband and children is pouring through my hands, into the bread which will not only refresh them after work and play, but will actually build the cells in their bodies.

For the rest of the day, I become aware of the difference between slopping through a task, and allowing love to pour through my hands. Awareness brings sweetening to the golden baking, a blessing on the vegetables I cut into the soup, satisfaction while stirring the tasty meal, patient problem solving while dressing the children, clever creativity with a craft project as I prepare an artistic greeting card and choose words to compose a letter to a friend.

Within these very real limitations, I still have a choice. My voice can scold, or convey love. My face and gestures can hang heavy, or move with brightness. Hugs and even waving

Wednesday, February 1, 1984

good-bye communicate love. Everyone knows that. But it takes a shift in concentration to feel it coming out of me on purpose. Necessary, routine, repetitive actions are enriched with meaning when I remember why and for whom I am doing the task.

Just as Kevin is getting up and I am ready to serve the soup and bread, there is a knock on the door. Rarely do we have guests. I open the door to see Bill Payne. He has come in from the mountains to ask Kevin to join him on the trap-line.

I am embarrassed to offer such a boring lunch to an unexpected guest.

The broth for the soup had been in the freezer. I saved the orange water from blanching carrots from the summertime garden. Chunks of leftover roast beef, diced potatoes, chopped green beans and carrots made for a pretty plain meal.

"That's a mighty fine mulligan!" Bill Payne commented on this hasty but tasty bowl of soup. He praised the warm bread, melted butter and honey, too.

With a preschooler and a toddler, I am constantly interrupted during the meal. I tune out the men's voices as they swap stories, make plans, exchange information and occasionally laugh.

The men move to sit in the living room, but I have to stay on schedule and get the children down for a nap.

Kevin is eager to learn from his Old Timer friend about the mountains and waterways, snowmobiles, wildlife, trapping, topography, history, WWII, and survival skills. He listens intently to all the fire-fighting, parachuting, mountain man stories Bill Payne has to share. Together, they have spent many snowy days on the mountain and have a bond of mutual trust and friendship that is valued and rare.

While the men's voices continue and the children relax into sleep, I continue my thoughts, puzzling over my options. Surely there are things I can do to improve my own life while still accomplishing the on-going obligations I have to my family?

↘↓↙

How eagerly I await that first snowfall, hope for a white Christmas, look forward to winter sports. Winter Wonderland is endlessly beautiful as the branches are laden, the sky is bright blue, a breeze shimmers glittery snowflakes in the sunshine. Icicles, frost and animal tracks are Nature's decor.

But, seriously. Enough is enough! Each time the roads are clear, the temperature goes up and the calendar inches forward, I get my hopes up that we are DONE! And then: more white stuff. Sigh.

I know as a fact that time is passing. Still. It's hard to believe it will *ever* be Spring!

The woodshed is getting empty. The potatoes are running out. I watch too much TV. I've managed to stay fit (sort of). But it feels like an endurance test. "When are we going to get there?" the kids used to whine to Daddy on a long car trip. It reminds me of when Bambi complained during his first winter, cold and hungry. His Mother said, "It seems long, but it won't last forever."

Volunteering helps. I receive a boost of energy when I give. Maybe I could have the preschoolers come to my house while the Moms do the fitness? Maybe Tuesdays and Thursdays. Maybe it's time to start having Sunday School, too. That would make three days per week. At least I will have little people around.

Words help. Reading, speaking and listening. Keeping a journal. Writing letters. Word games and puzzles. These keep the brain active and signal 'satisfaction.'

Wednesday, February 1, 1984

Animals help. Our fluffy black and white cat, Domino, and black lab, Tracker, make me realize that 'someone is happy to see me.'

Curiosity helps. Look. Listen. Ask. Learn. Reaching outside my everyday routine brings a kind of sunshine to the soul.

While the children nap, and I snooze, I ponder my gloomy situation from another perspective.

Ancient cultures repeat sacred ceremonies to bring back the sun. It's life and death! Think of it: Egypt, Mesopotamia, Aztec, Australia, Inuit, Norse, the Far East, the many peoples of Africa... they all had explanations, gods and goddesses, ritual robes, fires and sacrifices to coax the sun's return. Symbolic art work in caves, temples and tapestries indicate how universal this human need is to participate somehow in the changing seasons and return of the sun. The return of Life!

Maybe we should adapt traditions for our family during this time of year? What do we do less of or more of as the day-night ratio shifts? What foods or colours, outdoor activities or equipment, hobbies or interior decorations do I choose in wintertime and refresh with different choices in springtime?

The earliest stories preserved in the Bible also indicate a keen interest in how God provides for humankind through the predictability of the turning of the seasons.

In the first chapter of Genesis, verse 14, the Creator God says, "Let there be lights in the firmament of the heavens to separate the day from the night; and let them be for signs and for seasons and for days and for years." And, as if to renew the security and stability after the chaos of the flood, God speaks again (recorded in Genesis 8:22) "While the earth remains, seedtime and harvest, cold and heat, summer and winter, day and night, shall not cease."

Well. OK. God made it. I might be wise to quit complaining and accept it.

February Chapter 3

I think there is still time this winter for me to finish the hand stitching on the quilt I have been working on, even if it is a little bit at a time.

↘↓↙

I know one other thing I can do. I can add to my notebook of quotations. Words of wisdom always orient me and bring me out of the gloom and into the light.

> Enjoy what you do, and do it
> because you have something to give.
> The JOY in having something
> is sharing it with other people.
> *Marianne Tcherkassy*
> *American Ballet Theater*

> Life is 10% what happens to me
> and 90% how I react to it.
> *Charles Swindoll*

> To everything there is a season
> and a time for every purpose under heaven.
> A time to be born and a time to die;
> a time to break down, and a time to build up;
> a time to weep, and a time to laugh;
> a time to mourn, and a time to dance;
> a time to cast away stones,
> and a time to gather stones together;
> a time to embrace, and a time to refrain from embracing;

a time to seek, and a time to lose;
a time to keep, and a time to cast away;
a time to tear, and a time to sew;
a time to keep silence, and a time to speak;
a time to love, and a time to hate;
a time for war, and a time for peace.
Ecclesiastes 3:1-8

↘↓↙

What Happened Next?
Now that we live in town, I am invited to baby showers and Tupperware parties. I still feel like a newcomer, and I am so happy to meet all of the ladies. One-by-one I asked the women, "How do you cope with these long winters?" Marijuana, alcohol or antidepressants were used by many. One woman slept with a Bible on her chest.

I am 26 years old. What the more experienced, older women tell me is a little scary for me to comprehend. I feel determined to wrestle against this overwhelming seasonal cycle of depression and share whatever information that I find.

↘↓↙

For nine more years, I fumbled through the winter months. I wondered if medication and therapy might be part of my wellness plan?

I didn't know it then, but I know it now: Seasonal Affective Disorder (SAD) and Clinical Depression are real. A trip to the doctor is of value.

It takes courage to take a personal inventory and learn more about my own state of health.

Chapter 3
Saturday, March 17, 1984

To live a creative life
we must lose our fear
of being wrong.
   —Joseph Chilton Pearce

↖↑↗

Preschool in our house is going great.

Since we have running water, we can paint and do play-dough and clean up. Since there is a kitchen, we can do a few make-your-own-snacks. And since it is not so cold, we can play without snow pants on. The ladies in the fitness class are very thankful for me to volunteer to look after the children.

Everybody's happy.

Sunday School in the old log schoolhouse is going great.

Cheryl has been looking after Michael so he doesn't wreck the art project the school aged children are making. He's getting the idea of the routine at preschool now. Soon he can join in to Sunday School, too.

This is the routine: I tell the story, we act it out, learn a song, I quote some of the Bible text, we make a take-home craft, we work on a group project such as a mural, then we have worship at the end. We light the candles, then kneel to say the Lord's Prayer. I read the story from the Bible that we just learned. We recite the verse and sing the song that we learned about today's story. Then we bow our heads and ask the Lord to help us remember what we learned today.

Last Christmas, I directed a shadow play for the Christmas Concert at the Hall. All of the teenagers participated. We hung three white sheets across the whole width of the room. I used a desk lamp to cast shadows. The audience was hushed as the angel appeared, Mary and Joseph laid the Baby in the manger, the shepherds knelt, the Wise Men opened their gifts. Kevin read from Luke and Matthew while the actors held their pose. I played the guitar and led hymns in-between scenes. I did not realize until after the last scene that the audience was packed! People who had visitors brought their guests! Kevin estimated that 70 people were there!

I have Sunday School lesson plans for Easter. I found a hollow log in the woodshed. I can make a little scene to show the children the story. I already have the small dolls we used to act out the story of Adam and Eve. I will use them for Mary at the empty tomb when she saw Jesus in the garden.

For Mother's Day we will decorate paper plates and cups and paper napkins and invite the Moms to come for a luncheon at the Community Hall. Meanwhile, I will give the Moms a script to practice a skit.

Saturday, March 17, 1984

↖↑↗

Two months ago, in mid-January, I decided to go to the monthly town meeting to see if I could volunteer to form a committee and start something new. I proposed to organize a Family Fun Event once a month. (No alcohol) I asked for a $50 'purse' that I could spend for what ever supplies were needed. If we charge admission or sell tickets to win a prize, then we can draw the money back in to refill the purse.

Cheryl, Fran, Debbie and Opal came to the meeting. It was not too hard to convince them about my good idea. It won't be any kind of huge fundraiser, but it will give families something to look forward to and ways for families to participate in an outing together every month.

I am remembering the annual Family Fun Night we had in the Arbour Vale Church Community where I used to live in Ontario. Food and games, contests and guessing, little prizes, challenges, laughter. It was like an indoor carnival with booths for different activities.

I am bursting with eagerness. I have so many ideas: Spelling Bee, Baking Contest, Talent Night, Storytelling, Treasure Hunt, Slide Show of vacations and trips, Games and Puzzles, Bingo.

"We could have 'A Day in the Sun' as the first Fun Family Event," I suggested. The president, vice-president, secretary and treasurer's face were blank. The Recreation Society made more use of the Community Hall with dances and parties for adults. A liquor license was easier to ask for than the Family Fun that I was suggesting.

Cheryl was sitting beside me. She had a lot more experience with these monthly community meetings, so she took over the pitch.

"What Eleanor is envisioning is a Family Fun Fair. There would be booths like apple bobbing, pin-the-tail-in-the-donkey, guessing games and a bean bag toss. It would also be a potluck, but instead of casseroles and pies there would be summertime foods like carrots and celery, potato salad and watermelon. We could set up a Bar-B-Q out in the parking lot to roast hot dogs. Iced tea and lemonade would help set the theme."

I take up the proposal. "The thing is, winter is so long. Not everyone can make that snowbird trip to Arizona! But, if we invited everyone to dress in their summer clothes and decorated the Hall as if it was tropical... we could even have Caribbean or surfer music playing. It would be fun!"

A few smiles were forming, people were making eye contact, checking to see if there was agreement.

"What would it cost?" Brenda, the ever practical treasurer, asked the obvious.

"Well, I've thought about that, too." Now I had to really dig deep for my courage. "Since we've moved into town, I have been volunteering at the school and trying to think of things for our families to do together. I would like to plan something once each month. Where I used to live in a similar sized community, there was a committee with a 'purse' of $50. It gets spent and refilled each time there is an event. In other words, it costs, say, $50 to put on an event, but the admission, or meal, or games, or whatever income is brought in would refill it each time. If there's extra income, it would be turned in, but if there was not quite enough, the Rec Committee would refill the purse. That way it would not be money just draining away."

"So, you're really asking for three things? One: a monthly Family Fun event. Two: a $50 purse. Three: a February event in the Hall. Is that correct?" Rhonda, the president, was so practical and clear. A business woman and involved with local government, her skills keep our town informed and orderly.

Fran, Brenda and Rhonda, are empty-nesters, can't really see how they might be involved. But Opal, who is the vice-president, as well as Debbie, Cheryl and I have small children. And there are nearly 30 elementary school-aged children as well as teenagers. I just know how much fun we can all have together. But, I have to wait for the vote.

"Sounds like a good time to me," Opal offers.

Fran, the secretary, is everybody's favourite Grandma. Decisively she adds, "Let's give it a try. The worst thing that could happen is we spend $50 and nobody shows up. But in the middle of February, when we are all shut in, I think a family outing might be just dandy!"

Votes are cast, the 'Ayes' have it. $50 is in my hand. I have a new role in the community and a new project every month and the very first date on the calendar. February 18th is 'Family Fun.'

↖↑↗

In the weeks that followed I asked other mothers for ideas, talked at the post office with neighbours, met up with the teenagers after the school bus arrived at 4:30. Most importantly, I started writing lists.

A poster at the community bulletin board near the post office and another one at the Log Inn Pub announced the theme, date, time and admission. Phone calls gave more specific instruction: summer clothes, picnic foods, bring a lawn chair.

People thought I was nuts, but that's OK. They sounded hesitant, but by word-of-mouth the idea started to gain momentum.

A travel agent donated out-of-date posters of tropical destinations and holiday resorts, palm trees along white beaches and surfers catching the waves.

The Grade 7 and 8 students made a large, round, yellow paper maché pinata filled with peanuts, wrapped caramels and wrapped hard candy.

The Grade 4, 5 and 6 students painted the mural which would be the backdrop for the portrait studio featuring gentle blue waves, golden sunset, sandy beaches, swaying green palm trees, hovering white seagulls, bright yellow sun shining down.

The Grade 1-2-3 children cut out travel catalogues and made a collage to decorate the entry.

All of the students took a renewed interest in studying the classroom globe.

The high school students pitched in, too. Wendy wanted to dress as a gypsy and made a booth in the dark storage space, hung fringe-trimmed curtains and prepared to 'tell fortunes.' Other teens signed up to come the day before to help decorate.

"Music! I forgot all about music! Who has a sound system that they would be willing to set up? What music would set the mood?" As the date grew closer, I got a little panicky.

"I'll look after that," Cheryl offered. "Jim does the dances all the time. He has tapes and a record collection you wouldn't believe. Beach Boys, Elvis... all kinds of party music from the '60s and '70s. He'd love to do it."

We interrupt each other with familiar tunes.

And we'll have fun fun fun
'til my Daddy takes the T-bird away!

California Girls, California Girls!

Do you love me? Do you surfer girl?

"Great! There's always Harry Belefonte! *My island in the sun...* and how about *Come mister tally man and tally me banana!*

Do you have those?" Those songs fill my imagination with Caribbean scenery.

"How about teaching the school kids a song or two?" Opal suggests.

"Hmm, I'll put on my thinking cap." It will have to be an easy one. It's almost time!

↖↑↗

"Are people going to come?" I checked in with Cheryl and Opal on Thursday when they dropped their kids off for preschool at my house.

"I think *everybody* is coming!" Cheryl grinned. "Getting the kids involved at school was a stroke of genius. Nobody will miss a production if the children are involved!"

"I agree, and the grandparents will come just to see the little ones' happy faces!" Opal added.

The day before the event the Hall was as busy as a bee-hive. Bob, the town handyman, had a ladder tall enough to hang the pinata from the ceiling's central beam. I bought lots of yellow streamers and the teens helped me radiate them out from the pinata to make a welcoming, glowing sun!

↖↑↗

On Saturday, February 18, 1984, the Community Hall looked inviting when the people arrived. Each of the small tables had become another booth.

In the middle of the room, under the yellow sun pinata, families set up a picnic style meal. Folding lawn chairs appeared. Picnic blankets were spread out. Children dodged here and there finding friends and coming and going as they do at any picnic. Wide brimmed floppy sun hats, dark sunglasses, colourful dresses, shorts and even bathing suits and beach towels brought the scene to life. Some people were wearing turtle neck sweaters and long johns underneath their long, flowing sun dresses.

The teacher, Mrs. Olson, even brought a bottle of suntan lotion and passed it around. I could see the smiles on faces as the scent brought everyone even more deeply into the pretend we were all creating.

People shared what they had brought. The long tables held iced tea and lemonade served in brightly coloured plastic glasses with tall straws. Pickles and carrot sticks, banana bread and slices of melon, coleslaw and potato chips, potato salad and pineapple slices all brought colours and smells totally unexpected in the winter white.

While the music played, the menfolk braved the cold outdoors to roast the hot dogs on the BBQ. Everyone gathered around when they brought in the platter heaped with savoury meat. The hot dogs smelled great. Buns were dripping with ketchup and mustard and relish. Big grins were everywhere.

Families explored the booths. Even the older people participated in the guessing games.

What is the distance from Avola to Fiji? Arizona? Hawaii?

How many coffee beans are in this jar?

What is the weight of this bag of bananas?

What are warmest and coldest temperatures recorded in the Bahamas?

The children played 'Pin the Coconut on the Tree' and enjoyed a bean bag toss with a happy clown face target. The Gypsy had lots of customers lined up. Hooting and hollering came from the apple bobbing barrel. Patricia, with the Polaroid camera, almost missed eating all together. Everyone wanted their portrait taken.

Saturday, March 17, 1984

Some teenagers volunteered to man the booths, some helped little ones with their games, some had practised an 'Air Band' routine and everyone laughed at their gyrations and comedy efforts.

As a Grande Finale, the folding chairs and picnic blankets were cleared away. A mop handle and blindfold were provided as one-by-one, from youngest to oldest, the children took turns whacking at the pinata. A swing and a miss. A swing and a thud. The round yellow sun became battered and torn, but still held the candy. A little discouraged, the teenagers were getting turns. And then, all at once, a shower of candy, peanuts, pennies and balloons spilled onto the floor. Scrambling and clutching their treasures, the children ended the event with a satisfaction that made even the bystanders leaning against the wall feel the warmth of community.

And, to top it off, $150 was raised!

That first February Family Fun Event went so well that is was easy to convince neighbours to participate in another family function in March.

↖↑↗

Today, Saturday, March 17, we are having a Family Fun Event Baking Contest.

There are five categories: Bread, Pies, Cookies, Cakes and Junior Baker. Contestants signed in privately on a chart that others could not see. Each entry has little numbered flags. Helpers deliver the baked goods to a long table in front of the stage.

Each time a new category is presented, three new Judges are called to the stage, blindfolded and given a plate with samples on it to taste.

Laughter fills the Hall.

Meanwhile, at another table, bowls of white powders are of interest to contestants. It is a guessing game. Who can correctly name the ingredients? Sugar, salt, corn starch, milk powder, white flour, icing sugar, baking powder, baking soda. They all look so much alike!

Prizes are awarded for each category: measuring cups, aprons, tea-towels, pot holders. Every contestant is given recipe cards which had been obtained by writing to the various companies that produced cocoa, molasses, raisins, corn starch, baking powder, flour, and other ingredients.

All of the remaining baked goods are put up for sale and the pies are sold by the slice so everyone can stay for refreshments.

Good times. Community Spirit. Family Fun!

↖↑↗

What Happened Next?

In May, 1984, an historic School Board meeting was held at the Avola School. The decision was passed unanimously to close the school.

By the time September arrived, most families had moved away.

It was the end of an era.

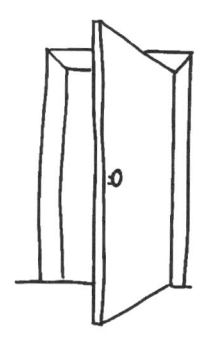

Chapter 4
Monday, February 9, 1987

Depression on my left,
and loneliness on my right.
They don't need to show me their badges.
I know these guys very well.
— *Elizabeth Gilbert*

↘↓↙

Christmas is over. Spring is a long way off.

As usual, February is a tricky month for me.

I know that. My husband knows that. The kids are too small to realize my difficulty. I have to be careful not to spill my discomfort out onto them. Interruptions and disobedience, their needs and hurts, unending questions and frequent misbehaviour are perfectly normal for their stage of development, and not intended to provoke my limited patience.

To complicate matters, I am pregnant. Sleepy. Hungry. Hormonal. Swollen. Heavy.

To make matters worse, my Oma passed away last week. It takes time to realize that someone so important is gone. My Mother, two aunts and two uncles were with her for her last days in Colorado. It is a strange sensation to await with joy the arrival of Oma's new descendant that I carry within me, while at the same time I grieve the loss of the Matriarch of our family. I am 29 years old, but I feel the pressure of time. Nobody knows how many days they have left on this Earth.

I cling to my husband as he leaves for work. For eight hours he will be alone, in the dark, inspecting miles of snowy track through the rock cuts. A hard hat, a head lamp, a radio, a kerosene lamp, a lunch box, a reflective vest are his provisions and protection as he peddles through the wilderness. Silently my eyes memorize his face. Will I see him tomorrow?

This year the gloomy, repetitive, no-end-in-sight part of the winter seems more challenging while the baby growing inside me claims my air and food and interrupts my sleep. My feet and hands are swollen. My back aches. I have to pee again and again all night. I am hungry all the time. My clothes are too tight. I fell asleep yesterday while the kids had the TV on. Sometimes I just wish I was someplace else. Someplace where there is extended family, friends or servants to look after everyone and everything so that I could just be me. I have enough problems and needs of my own. But, my husband and children are still expecting to have the usual domestic tasks done by me.

Kevin came home early this frosty morning after patrolling the train tracks through the night. So quietly (he knows I want every moment of sleep for myself), he ate some toast and slid into bed. I curled up against his back, offering warmth. My hugely round belly makes it hard to cuddle, but then, cuddling is how this baby began.

Soon he sleeps. Soon the children will wake. I have a few moments. Quiet. Alone. Thinking. Planning.

Monday, February 9, 1987

↘↓↙

"What can I do with what I have?"

I realize and appreciate the resources I have collected and send a little prayer of thanksgiving up to the Provider.

The woodshed is comfortably full. I am thankful to be warm with no worries about rationing wood. The tally of garden produce in the freezer is still generously supplying our meals with peas and corn, beans and spinach, Swiss chard and beets, raspberries, blackberries, blueberries, Saskatoon berries, apple sauce, peaches, plums and plenty of rhubarb. Bear meat and venison have been brought in from the forest. The cellar holds baskets of potatoes, shelves of canned soup from the store and jars of homemade pickles and jam. The pantry has glass jars of beans, rice, barley, oats, raisins, nuts, peanut butter, cornmeal, bags of flour and sugar. The refrigerator has cheese and milk, eggs and yogourt. There is plenty to choose from to plan a menu for the day.

I think I'll bake today. It is both a necessity and it passes the time, and it gives me a sense of accomplishment. The children like to help and learn. Michael is a champion at making granola. Besides, granola is not an exact science. He can scoop the oats, dump in sunflower seeds and coconut, stir the mixture and dribble in the melted oil and honey. Elise can stand on a block of wood at the stove top and stir the melty chocolate no-bake cookies and drop the spoonfuls onto a tray to cool. But first, I'll start the bread dough rising, so that by the time the granola is out of the oven and I pop in a pan of muffins, we can knead the bread dough. The children like to make shapes with the bread dough, or add cheese and onions, or sometimes raisins and cinnamon, or make a bun for their Daddy's lunch.

There is one more benefit of baking today. It will give me an excuse to go visit Barb Liscumb. I could certainly use an outing. By the time the bread is out of the oven, Kevin will be awake. He can take a turn looking after the children while I go out visiting.

I have been focused on organizing every single part of our four-room house. Some people say it's the 'Nesty' part of the pregnancy. But, I have developed this annual part of the cycle, after I put the Christmas decorations away, to best use the January-February months. There's nothing to do outside except shovel snow and carry firewood. And, at this stage of my pregnancy, I should probably avoid both. So, I devote my time to either making a mess or cleaning messes up.

Most of my neighbours wait until late March or early April to do their Spring Cleaning. After months of wood smoke, soot and bits of bark in the house, they wash walls and scrub everything in sight. The longer daylight makes it easier to see the places which need attention, including the windows. The warmer weather means the doors can be left open for traffic in and out while rugs are taken up to be beaten, bedding is hung outside, cobwebs are swept from rafters, floors are scrubbed. Switching winter coats and boots for summer gear is another part of the chore.

I have been working my way through each room.

In the children's room, I have been emptying drawers one-by-one, sorting clothing and toys, putting away things that are too small. What can be used when this baby grows? What things can be bagged up to take to the Thrift Store?

In our room, which used to be for a work bench and tools, Kevin built us a high bed. I have room to store about twelve boxes under the bed. There is no attic, storage shed or garage, so this is the solution to make more storage in such a small house. Winter boots and coats switch for summer clothes. Christmas ornaments switch for croquet and Frisbees.

Monday, February 9, 1987

Kevin's Mom sends us another box from Ontario almost every month. She has a Thrift Store less than a block away from where she lives. She has asked the volunteers there to save us any educational toys, such as maps, music, books, puzzles, building sets and craft items. She also sends clothing, winter gear and handy kitchen gadgets. She really likes to shop for birthday decorations. She has previously provided Rainbow Bright, Garfield, Care Bears, and Get-Along-Gang hats, tablecloths and prizes for goodie bags.

With the limited resources we have available to us in this tiny town, I am so grateful for the way she provides for us.

As I organize, I also have been cleaning the bedrooms. I like to put on cassette tapes of music as an encouragement. Vacuum. Dust. Wash windows. Change the sheets. Maybe if I move the furniture, it will cheer up the room. I'm sure I have fabric to make more colourful curtains.

In the living room there is Kevin's desk to organize, book shelves to straighten and dust. I vacuum behind the couch and under the cushions. Is there a better way to arrange the furniture? Is there a better way to cover the couch? Maybe I'll bring some colour with the Oma afghan or different pillows?

The bathroom won't take long. Barrettes and lotions and First Aid supplies each have their place. I can straighten the towels and scrub each fixture. I am still so thankful that we no longer have an outhouse. I am so glad for the propane hot water tank!

Elise was born when we lived in the cabin. Michael was born when we lived in the stackwall. It seems like a trend: New House - New Baby! Now that we live in town, this will be the first time I have a bathtub instead of a basin to wash my new baby!

I try to tidy up and sweep in the front hall where the boots and coats are at least once a week. It is important with growing children to try on pairs of shoes and boots to see if anything is outgrown. Other jobs I try to keep up on are the laundry (I wash a load in the evening and hang it up to dry overnight on a string above the wood stove), refrigerator (I clean out every two weeks before payday shopping), the freezer (which I empty and scrub every spring before I start to harvest rhubarb), and the back porch (where the firewood is stacked).

It's a dreary cycle if I start to feel sorry for myself. "Am I the only one around here qualified to wash the dishes?" I grumble. "For this I went to college?" I mutter. If I was still in the city with a career, maybe I'd pay someone to look after this kind of work. But then, I wouldn't be married to Kevin, nor would I be a stay-at-home-Mom. I'd also be paying for daycare and missing the daily progress, learning, explorations and clever surprises that happen each day.

Maybe today, I can get the kitchen organized since I'll be there making the bread and other baking. If I can enlist the children to help, it can be part of our homeschooling today. While I am scrubbing out the drawers and cupboards, Elise, nearly seven, can read aloud. She has learned a little French from Sesame Street. I can ask Michael, age five, the sounds of each letter. We can count. We can look for shapes and colours. We can sing songs. I can supervise a game of Simon Says.

Last time we had a baking day with cleaning combined, I said, "I am going to be Cinderella. You be my mouse-friend helpers." But, then they disappeared! I started to moan dramatically and sigh longingly. "I wish I had a little help with all this work! I hope I can go to the Prince's Ball in the Castle." I wondered where they went and what they were doing?

Then, the bedroom door opened. Two rascally faces peeked out. "We are Good Fairies. You can't see us. These are our Magic Boots!" Elise and Michael had wrapped paper and tape around their feet and ankles. Silently (except for a few giggles) the work was done - as if by magic.

Monday, February 9, 1987

↘↓↙

Without the pressure of the clock, I can schedule the homeschooling day to suit the ebb and flow of energy, interest and interruptions. If I lift my mind above the limitations, I can see the possibilities.

Other ideas start to pop into my mind.

I see some people who need haircuts. We could make an event out of it, role playing, pretending to be preparing for a party or a ball. Yes, the dress-up clothes haven't been out for awhile.

Today will be the last day of Spring Cleaning, so tomorrow we could have a craft day. Get out of the books and make a big mess. See where our creativity and curiosity will lead us.

Most importantly, today, I have another reason to be focusing on making our house clean and tidy. Besides the usual cycle of the year, besides the preparations for the new baby, the good news is, my Mother is coming! She will be here for the birth!

↘↓↙

I hear Elise and Michael waking up now. And so, the day begins. First, there is a flurry of morning activity, then a lull while the two hours of the kids' daily TV shows gives me a break. Fred Penner is the new guy. *The Cat Came Back* is so much fun to sing. Sharon, Lois and Bram sing on the 'Elephant Show.' They always end their program by singing the same song.

Skin-a-ma-Rinky-Dinky-Dink,
Skin-a-ma-Rinky-Do.
I love you!

Kevin is available to watch the children during lunch and naps. So, I can step around the corner and take Barb Liscumb a plate of goodies from our baking.

↘↓↙

Barb Liscumb lives alone in a little blue house. She is a retired teacher who has lived in many parts of Canada. She no longer drives, so Fran and Cheryl, Jennie and Cecile take turns looking after her grocery list. I first met her at the Community Hall Christmas Concert three years ago. Fran went to pick her up, walking carefully beside her while she slowly made her way along the snowy path with her crutches. Her big smile was shining while the children were singing, the Nativity scene was portrayed, and later when Santa called each child to sit on his lap.

Because I have been directing skits, playing the guitar and chasing my own children, I haven't actually talked to her until this Christmas. She called me over and with twinkling eyes, thanked me for the way I played *Silent Night*. We talked about my Sunday School and she invited me to come and borrow some books she used to use when she was teaching in a Catholic school.

Since then, for the last two months, I have made a point of stopping in for a visit, to bring goodies, or to ask if I can bring her anything when we go to town on payday. She has the strangest grocery list. 8 large boxes of Cheerios, 12 cans of mushroom soup, 3 large boxes of Saltine crackers, 3 bottles of Sunlight dish soap. Maybe three or four items, but always in large quantities. She explained to me that if she sends a complicated grocery list, the helpful neighbour might omit or mistake something, then she has none. But, if she stays stocked up and sends a list of only a few items, then her needs are met without pressure on the helpful neighbour.

I knock on the blue door and hear the crutches and single boot slowly approach. "It's me, Eleanor!" I call so she is not startled.

"Oh, my!" she exclaims when the blanket-curtain is pulled back and the door swings open. "Look who's here!" She welcomes me in to her little winter home.

She seems to live in one room. Grey metal utility shelves have been set up as partitions. This makes the space she tries to heat even smaller and more compact. She gestures for me to sit on an easy chair, arranges her skirts and shawls and blankets to return to her warm seat on the couch. She rolls the upright electric heater closer to me and offers me a paper mat to put under my feet. The single electric bulb above us shines into this cube of space, but leaves the rest of the room behind the shelves in shadow.

"The bread is still warm!" Her eyes sparkle a thank-you. She covers the loaf with both hands, warming them. Like the characters in Dickens' Christmas carol, she wears finger-less gloves, wraps a woollen scarf around her head and shoulders, her plaid kilt hiding the shorter leg, the single booted foot warmed by long pants and thick socks. Her eyes are bright, always grateful for every small good thing that comes her way.

"I can cut you a slice now," I offer, scanning the further places to see if there is a kitchen counter available. "I brought butter and honey, too."

She produces a cutting board and serrated knife from the shelf at her right elbow, a plate from the shelf below and I am able to arrange things on my lap to make her a snack. Silently, eyes closed, she savours the crispy crust, warm bread and the melting, delicious, honey mingled with butter.

The electric heater feels good and I hold my hands above the coils. The paper mat she has made by weaving folded newspapers, adds some insulation between the floor and her boot. I don't ask questions about her lifestyle. We are both more eager to have an intelligent conversation. She turned the small black and white TV off before she answered the door. I always hope I am not interrupting her favourite show, or news, or movie.

"How are the children?" she always asks. Then, "How is your husband?" and also, "How is the Sunday School?"

It is wonderful to share my observations, accomplishments and thoughts with someone. It is wonderful to share personal glimpses and family stories with someone who is not going to gossip or distort my meaning. Most wonderful of all, she believes in the importance of the Sunday School and the significance of my efforts to bring the most basic knowledge of the Bible and introduce the love of Jesus to the children in this remote mountain village. She listens intently. She looks for the good. She guides from experience. She appreciates humour. She speaks with depth and sympathizes with the problems I am struggling with. She realizes the challenge to have my family dedicated to the Lord in a place where faith is rare, Bible knowledge almost unknown, and religion mostly shunned. It makes my life very lonely, and time with her very precious.

I see the clock, and let her know what time I have to leave. She passes me a glass jar. "Take a few mints home for the children," she coaxes me. "I found this book. Would you like to borrow it?" I see that she has been ready, hoping I would come. This old textbook has pictures of Bible stories the children will enjoy.

Although she lives with so little, she always gives me so much.

Monday, February 9, 1987

↘↓↙

On my way home, pushing my heavy winter boots through four inches of new snow, I feel a familiar sensation. I stop and pay attention to the contraction. It passes quickly. However, from now until the baby is born, whenever I bend, lift, wear winter boots, or make any effort at all, a contraction will remind me to stop. This first warning brings a significant change to our family structure. From now on, my husband or children will move the vacuum cleaner, reach into the washing machine for wet laundry, stretch to hang it up and pull it down when it's dry. Carrying grocery bags, firewood, garbage bags, boxes for the Thrift Store are all no longer in my range of activity.

I relay the enjoyment of my time with Barb, and share my concern with Kevin about the contractions. He needs to go back to sleep. I read aloud to Elise and Michael.

↘↓↙

There is a knock on the door. I put the kettle on for my guest. It's the Town Busy-Body. Relaying stories of the neighbours, passing on advice, sticking her nose into family matters. Usually I am guarded, keep my comments brief, try not to state an opinion, remain neutral. Above all, I block myself from sharing anything personal. But today, I'm happy for a female friend and the wealth of having two conversations in one day, I shoo the children into the living room and get them started on building a town with their blocks.

Eager to confide in someone, I spill out the depressing realization that my growing belly is not all easy, there is still a month to go, and I will be able to do less, which means boredom and empty days. "And, secretly, I am jealous of my husband." Her eyebrows go up. I spill out my emotions, "He gets to go to work. He talks to people every day. He goes snowmobiling with friends. He can lift and work and make an effort and have the satisfaction of a job well done." I can't find words to convey my frustration and disappointment. "I feel so fat and tired. Like a sloth. I feel jealous of all the ladies with a waist-line, wearing make-up, with their hair done. I just want to be glad about having a baby, but I also feel... blue." I look at her hopefully, ears straining, expecting a word of comfort or practical experience.

"Sex is the answer," she bluntly states. "Now, what was the question?" looking straight into my eyes.

Aghast, swollen and exhausted, grumpy and overflowing with self-pity, my hand instantly reaches across the table to slap her surprised face. Sex! Not really her business! How dare she speak such a thing?

"I think it's time for you to go," I recover some composure, hand over her coat, and shut the door, wondering what kind of story that will become when she gossips with the next neighbour?

↘↓↙

I turn to start supper, but then I hear a car in the driveway.

"The Bible Study Ladies are here!" Michael announces as he looks out the window.

It is amazing for me to have so many people to talk to in one day!

These are two of Jehovah's Witnesses who have been coming fairly often. I am always so glad to talk with anyone about the Bible. Besides the topic they want to cover, I also have been sharing my story, problems, and gloomy wintertime feelings.

"We can't stay long," Gail begins. "But we found these two Scriptures we thought you might find encouraging."

Monday, February 9, 1987

Susan is passing me a paper with her beautiful, smooth handwriting. "I find it so comforting to realize that I am not the only person having difficult experiences," she begins. "These ancient texts show us that emotions, troubles, and discouragement have been part of life and we are not alone if and when they come our way."

Thankful, I want to untangle my confusion. "Sometimes I wonder, 'What did I do to deserve this?' and I also have other thoughts of blaming myself," I confide.

As they drive away, I look closely at the note. It is always interesting to see how their translation of the Bible compares with the one I usually read.

> Jehovah is close to the broken hearted,
> He saves those who are crushed in spirit.
> Psalm 34:18

> For this is what the high and lofty one says
> who lives forever and His name is holy.
> I reside in the high holy place,
> but also with those crushed and lowly in spirit,
> to revive the spirit of the lowly,
> and to revive the heart of those being crushed.
> Isaiah 57:15

Now I can see that God does not bring trouble, but He does walk with us as we make our Journey.

↘↓↙

The sun is setting. Supper is simmering. The children are in the tub.

I take up my quilting for these few minutes of quiet. So much of keeping house is repetitive. Gone, with nothing to show for it. This way I will have accomplished something by the end of the day. By quilting, even a few stitches, using fabric I already have or cutting up old shirts, I am producing something permanent. The colours and geometrical arrangements satisfy my creativity without having to buy new materials.

So much of the work I do is invisible (correcting behaviour, teaching) or intangible (ethics, challenges, language development) unseen (no relatives, neighbours, friends near by) and repetitive (dishes, laundry, cleaning, wood, dog, cat). A quilt is something that will last, something I can see.

So much of the work I do is making things from scraps. Scraps! A little bit here and a little bit there. Tonight the supper is stew made from scraps of meat left on the bones. Scraps of vegetables I harvested from the garden, the last few peas on the dried up vines, tiny carrots, little cobs of corn I scraped off to save the golden kernels. The challenge of limitations and the abundance of scraps seem to be everywhere. Not only scraps of physical resources, but I might glean or waste scraps of time, money and other priorities that are important to me. How can I fit more fitness into my day? How can I stretch this pay cheque? How can I squeeze in more time to spend with my kids? It seems to me, if I notice little scraps, harvest them and value them, strive towards the goal and believe that 'something is more than nothing,' I might actually, little-by-little, achieve much.

Every winter, to spend the indoor days and early evenings, I challenge myself to use up a bin and a bag of fabric scraps. I wrestle with the limitations. I explore the possibilities. How shall I use this long strip of pastel? Bits and pieces of this rich green call to these floral prints. Four mismatched, yet complementary squares might be framed with these solids. How will

Monday, February 9, 1987

I ever bring unity and peace to this loudly shouting pile of orange, turquoise, purple and bright pink scraps?

I feel so satisfied when, like puzzle pieces, the quilt squares fit together.

↘↓↙

Tubby time is over. The children smell so clean and look so cozy in their PJs.

"Bedtime!" I call. "It's seven o'clock!"

"Toilet. Teeth. Book. Bed." That is our routine.

Scraps. Organization. Repetition. That's my routine.

At 10:00pm, Kevin's alarm clock goes off. He has a routine, too.

↘↓↙

What Happened Next?

Quilts have continued to be my primary hobby. I enjoy collecting fabric. I enjoy looking through patterns in library books and magazines. I enjoy the variations and possibilities and imagination and creativity. Maybe this? Maybe that? I enjoy the planning, the math, the measuring, the precision. I enjoy the cutting and sewing and gradually seeing the dream become a reality. I enjoy savouring the love I feel for the person I am making the quilt for. Sometimes memories are stirred up when I see the clothing I have cut up for the squares. My eyes are so happy from the colourful textiles while I work on the project through these monochromatic grey winter days. I enjoy basting the layers together, the hand stitching and hemming the edge. I enjoy the way the new quilt changes the look of the room. And, at last, I enjoy the sensation of warmth on a cold winter's night.

Chapter 4
Tuesday, March 31, 1987

> If there is beauty in the character
> there will be harmony in the home.
> If there is harmony in the home
> there will be order in the nation.
> If there is order in the nation
> there will be peace in the world.
> —Author Unknown

↖↑↗

"Youch! What was that?"

My Mother is a massage therapist. She is giving me a foot reflexology treatment. She explains to me. "Each pressure point on the sole of the foot is connected to an organ or function of the body. When each point is stimulated with the pressure of my hands, the organ is encouraged to perform it's function. For instance, if you have tired eyes, you can gain relief by pressing here (she presses between my second and third toe). If you have a sore throat, healing can come more quickly if you stimulate here (where the big toe meets the sole of the foot). If you are experiencing constipation, it helps to rub and press firmly here (across the sole near the heel end of the arch)." Sounds interesting. There's really no way I can confirm or deny this, but I am happy to enjoy the attention and her skill. "If there is a sharp sensation, the therapist can tell the client what organ they are stimulating. The client may not be aware of distress, but the body knows there is a problem. For instance, you have no nerves to signal pain in the liver, so problems may be there already, but undetected. Reflexology can both identify problems and begin to call the body to self-heal through this kind of massage." I don't know if I believe it, but it sure feels nice.

Mother has been at our house for just over a month waiting for this baby to be born. She has been giving me marvellous head rubs, back rubs, hand and foot rubs. So far this foot rub feels very soothing as she presses deeply into the joints and muscles, explores the tendons, nerves and circulation. The scent of the lotion and trust I have for her nurturing touch is very relaxing. Everything feels very nice.

Suddenly. This jolt! It seems alarming.

"Mom, seriously, what part of my body are you finding on my foot?" I have pulled my foot away from her, the sensation is sharp and unpleasant. I am surprised to see her big grin. And even more surprised by her answer.

"That's you're uterus!" We both laugh.

My uterus has been stretched so large by this pregnancy. Small contractions have been occurring for over a month. The due date came and went nearly two weeks ago.

In fact, today is the last day Doctor Lam is allowing me to 'wait and see' if labour will begin naturally. Tomorrow I will have to go to Kamloops to be induced. It is hazardous for the baby to remain inside too long. The placenta begins to be less efficient in conveying nutrients to the unborn child. I have tried several of the suggested ways to 'shake that baby out,' including long walks, a hot then suddenly cold shower and raspberry leaf tea. The Doctor even suggested that intercourse can stimulate hormones to begin stronger contractions. So far, no progress.

Maybe foot reflexology will do the trick. I give my foot back for another pressurized session. It doesn't feel very good, but, since it is so very different from any other part of the care, I am convinced that there is something true about this therapeutic method.

"I'm so glad you're here." Our eyes meet and we both realize we are entering each other's life story in an entirely new way. She was, after all, there when I was born! She has recently been present at the deathbed of her own mother, my Oma. Now she will witness the birth of her grandchild. I feel the mingling of hope and fear. No one knows what lies ahead.

↖↑↗

Dearma came to visit last summer in June, 1986. She drove with a lady friend all the way up from Florida, visiting relatives all along the way. Elise and Michael enjoyed her visit so much that they hid her car keys to delay her departure.

We have been sending photos, writing letters, mailing art work and homemade cards all year. Since there is a three-hour time zone difference and long distance telephone calls are free before 8:00am, we can also talk on the telephone frequently. My siblings don't have children yet. These are her only grandchildren so far.

So, when she decided to come again in late February, 1987, it seemed so soon. Elise and Michael were very excited.

"Let's surprise her!" Elise got the idea. "Michael can wear my pink and blue snow suit and I'll wear his brown one! She won't know which one is which!"

We waited up beside the highway, near the gas station. Dearma was coming on the Greyhound from Vancouver.

"The bus! I see the bus!" Michael was jumping and waving.

Dearma stepped down the stairs and was immediately wrapped with small people's hugs and great big grins.

"Did we trick you?" Elise asked as we settled in.

"Will you read to us?" Michael had a favourite story picked out that I had recently read more than once.

"This is the story of 'Ali Baba and the Forty Thieves'... Ooo It sounds scary!" Dearma was in the middle, as the two snuggled up on either side.

I felt my heart sing to see the people who I love being so happy together. However, they looked so cozy, I might not get any time with Mother all to myself! I smiled and also pouted... just a little.

↖↑↗

The days since Dearma's arrival have been so much fun. She is interested in homeschooling and adds to the reading, writing, spelling, and math. She opens our bird book and describes what she sees in Florida. She comes with us to Clearwater and finds treasures in the grocery and hardware stores. She starts her own sewing projects and soon Elise has an embroidered night gown and Michael has a Canada flag patch sewn on his coat.

It is even more fun to watch TV together. We have three channels on our small black and white TV. She asks the children questions about their shows. "Why is he called 'Mr. Dress-up'? Who is 'Fred Penner'? Why are 'Sharon, Lois and Bram' called

'The Elephant Show'?" These programs are Canadian content which she has never seen before. She likes the afternoon reruns that I like to watch. 'Fantasy Island' allows guests at a resort to have their wishes come true, often to discover that it would be better to return to their normal life. 'Quincy' is the coroner who identifies criminals with the evidence he discovers. She can also recommend which movies to be sure to tune in.

And, of course, the food she makes is much more delicious than my cooking. Roast chicken for Sunday Dinner. Stacks of pancakes. Creativity with salads.

With the extra help, I take on more ambitious projects. On bread baking day I search in the freezer for blueberries to simmer into jam. Meanwhile, we take turns shaking a jar of cream to make butter and whir peanuts in the blender to make peanut butter. It takes all morning! We made our own lunch!

Mother already knows Fran and Cheryl and I take her to meet Barb Liscumb. I am so glad my Mother has come to visit so many times and knows the people I interact with.

March 17

The Baby's due date is also Saint Patrick's Day.

"Let's play dress-up," I suggested. There was absolutely no indication that I was going into labour. I needed to distract myself from pacing and looking at the clock and wondering if every tiny twinge was 'a sign'. This is my third time. When you're in labour, you know it.

The dress-up clothes are in a colourful, jumbled heap across the living room floor.

"We can be fairies and elves," I suggest, thinking of Ireland and the folklore of the Little People.

"Will you tie this?" Elise has a long pink robe.

"Would you like these gloves?" Dearma suggests.

"Is this hat good?" Michael wants to be an elf.

"How about this belt?" Dearma also finds a sturdy sack for the Gold and Treasure.

"We have to remember to wear something green! It's Saint Patrick's Day!" I explain about pinching.

Dearma allows the children to dress her. Kevin takes pictures when we are all dressed like fairies and elves, each with a sash or neck tie or head dress of green.

March 18

The due date has passed. I decide to thread soft, white yarn as the warp on my loom. As the days pass, I have a new project to occupy my time and keep my mind away from worries. Three red threads make a border along each of the four sides. It is a fringed baby blanket for my unborn child. Someday will I see a grandchild wrapped in it?

I am feeling anxious. Mother suggests daily walks. We go to the nearby creek. The next day we cross a meadow and hike up the hill. The warmer sunshine has caused the snow to melt by day and muddy puddles become ice by night.

Waiting. Waiting. No matter what else I am doing, I am still waiting.

There are so many unknowns during pregnancy. Kevin is still away all night as patrolman on the railroad. I am so glad Mother is here. Elise and Michael call to their sibling, put their hands on my belly, feel the kicking, sing songs and invite this person to come out and play.

March 31

Today, after the stimulating foot therapy, perhaps the contractions have changed? Before I go to bed, I get ready to go. Yes, at

5:00am a real signal. "Mother," I nudge her. "The water broke." I make a phone call to another railroad worker to contact Kevin on the radio. He's home in less than an hour.

Kevin takes Elise and Michael to Cheryl's house. Mother drives me to the Clearwater hospital in a big, tan station wagon borrowed from a neighbour for the occasion.

"It's just a ten-bed hospital," I explain to Mother as we drive along. It takes 45 minutes to get there. "Three rooms are for maternity patients." The building is constructed from portable units. One wing is for offices and meeting rooms. One wing has a room for the emergency / birthing / minor surgery, which ever is needed. There is a room for x-ray equipment and the kitchen to prepare meals for a maximum of ten patients. One wing is for the patients' rooms. The lab work and laundry are sent away.

As we sign in, I see a warning glance between the staff. It's my third birth. They think I'll be quick. I'm already fourteen days overdue and I've already been in labour for several hours! But, why are they alarmed? I feel fine. Then I hear another mother giving birth. There is not enough staff or space for two deliveries at the same time!

"I hope she's done before it's my turn!" I mutter to my Mother as we settle in.

But, I have made a slow start. Not much progress, but at least I am not going to Kamloops. I so much hope I can avoid having labour induced.

"You and your mother may go for a walk," Doctor Lam speaks to me in a confident manner.

We go way down the road. We sit on a bench to enjoy the view overlooking the old part of town, the river and the mountains across the valley. We go wandering through an empty lot. I stop to breathe deep and slow while a contraction passes through my muscles. We laugh and talk and I drink in the day.

Today is my child's birth day! A boy? A girl? It is exciting to wonder.

Eventually, we return to the hospital.

The nurses are anxious that we didn't come right back. But, I have made little progress.

The family has come to meet the new baby who was born this morning. It's a boy! The room is crowded. The father is beaming. The mother explains to me, "We have five daughters! This is our first son!" In an East Indian family, this is very significant and I am glad for them.

All of a sudden I realize that in five or six years, when they go to school, our children will know each other!

Evening. Still not much progress. Doctor Lam says I will have to go to Kamloops in the morning. Kevin goes to sleep at a friend's house. Mother sleeps in a chair down the hall. I continue to labour.

I didn't really want a St. Patrick's Day baby. Now I am hoping I don't have an April Fools Day baby! I am aware of the time.

Now it's past midnight in Newfoundland.

Now it's past midnight in Quebec.

Now it's past midnight in Winnipeg.

Now it's past midnight here.

March 31st is over.

What Happened Next?

April 1

I am in the bathroom.

I ring for the nurse.

"Do you feel like bearing down, pushing?"

"Yes," I gasp and pant, to slow things down until we are ready.

Tuesday, March 31, 1987

Quickly, she helps to get me back up on the bed. Examine me. Yes. Fully dilated. Call the Doctor. Call Kevin. Wake up Mother.

Onto the gurney. Wheel into the birthing room. Move over onto the table. I have been here before. "Sorry, Doctor Lam... it's the middle of the night... again!" I manage to grin between concentrated effort.

Previously, Mother had met Doctor Lam at a prenatal appointment. I told him, "She has recently midwifed her mother from this world to the next. Now she can midwife this child into this world. Such a very meaningful experience. This is her first time to witness a birth."

Doctor Lam invites my Mother to come and stand near him. They set up a mirror so I can see the baby's head crowning. Even Kevin is better prepared this time. I know what to do. I do not feel scared. I trust my own body. I trust Nature's forces. I trust everyone in the room. I feel the sacredness of the entire process. This baby was conceived knowingly and we asked the Lord for this gift. We have had such glad experiences with the older children. Cooperating with the forces of Nature, it feels great to be birthing. Everything works together.

Yes.

Yes.

And, here he is!

Doctor Lam hands the newborn to my Mother. Just a few breaths old, and already this new person turns to find my face when he hears my voice.

The nurse says, "It's Dad's turn now."

"Hello there, Buck Shot! Welcome to Planet Earth. I'm you're Dad. You have a big sister and a big brother and a dog and a cat and a fine Mother who will teach you many things. And, look! Dearma is here, too!"

Then, I get to hold him. So deeply warm and soft and smooth and pink and dear. Holding him to my left side, he eagerly finds the breast and nurses while the Doctor finishes his tasks and I am wheeled back to my room.

Kevin heads home to sleep.

Dearma waits until daylight, then drives all the way back to Avola to bring Elise and Michael all the way back to Clearwater to meet their brother. They have a picnic outside my window while Dearma comes in to see how I am doing. Then she is allowed to bring the two children into my room. This new little brother turns his head to find them. He recognizes their voices, too!

He recognizes their voices, too!

I don't have a camera!

Gail pops in. She offers to go get her camera. The moment is preserved!

After this special visit, just as they are all preparing to leave, Doctor Lam steps in and greets everyone.

When they walk down the hall, I follow. For a tiny moment, Doctor Lam puts his arm around my shoulders and says, "You have a lovely family." It makes me wonder, how many people he knows and how many little babies he has seen?

This is *my* family. This is the work *I* do.

I am so aware of the generations. Oma, Mother, me, our children, and someday, I hope to live to see the next generation.

I am so aware that what I am saying and doing will be remembered by these small people and their story will be woven with mine. "Dear Lord in Heaven, Help us, please, to provide for and protect, to love and teach these children You gave to us. Help us to help them know and love and follow You."

No more waiting. Nicholas is here. It is a very happy day.

Tuesday, March 31, 1987

↖↑↗

A little less than a year later, we moved again, still in Avola, now near the river.

A little over a year later, Toby was born and completed our family.

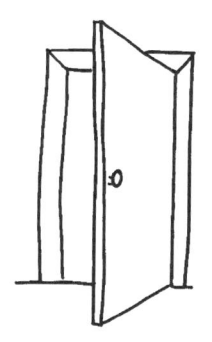

Chapter 5
Saturday, February 16, 1991

> It is very hard to explain to people
> who have never known serious depression or anxiety
> the sheer continuous intensity of it.
> There is no 'off' switch.
> —Matt Haig

↘↓↙

Here it comes again.
  These feelings are all too familiar.
  Midwinter Blues.
  I'm tired and droopy.
  I can't make up my mind about anything.
  The kids are driving me crazy. "I want this!" and "He took my that!" and "Can I do this?" and "He's not supposed to be doing that!" and "How come he gets such and such?"
  I say "No" a million times a day.
  I am mad at myself all the time.

February Chapter 5

I can't move.

I feel so heavy.

When I lift my arms I feel like I am lifting heavy suitcases. I see bedridden obese people on TV and I ask my husband, "Do I look like that?" I certainly feel too heavy to lift my own weight. I can't decide what to wear, so I wear the same clothes day and night for four days at a time. I feel like I am pushing a heavy wheelbarrow, or lifting a mattress, or struggling to move furniture. So, since it is too hard to stand up and walk across the room, I stay on the couch all day.

Doesn't anyone realize how hard it is to brush your teeth? Forget it. I'm not going to bother. I've thought it all out. First, you have to walk all the way over to the bathroom and push the heavy door shut. Then, you have to reach up to get your toothbrush and the heavy toothpaste tube. Next, you have to stand there for such a long time while you unscrew the cap. Squeezing the tube takes effort. Putting the cap back on takes extra energy. You get so tired standing there, for ages and ages shoving the foaming minty brush up and down, back and forth, keeping track of the left and right, front and back... It is all so exhausting. You lean against the sink while you wait for the warm water to come up from the basement because the cold water is such a terrible shock. More energy is lost while you finally rinse your mouth with warm water.

Ugh. No. I won't do it. It's just not worth it.

Then, if I actually do skip brushing my teeth, and after wearing the same clothes for four days, I get so mad at myself, all yucky and grimy. I decide to take a shower and clean up, but first, I have to stand in front of my dresser drawers and closet trying to decide what to wear. No matter what I pick I will have the unpleasant experience of cold clothing. Warming up my own clothes with my own body heat is just too hard to do.

Saturday, February 16, 1991

"I quit!" I say out loud to my husband. My face is droopy, my shoulders hunched, my voice a monotone. Everything is just too hard. "Today I punch my time card. I give my two weeks notice. I don't want to be a Mom anymore. I'm just too tired. Surely a 35 year old woman is not the only one who can decide what's for supper."

And I go back to lie down on the couch.

↘↓↙

The one thing I have to look forward to each week is going to the library. Yes! I actually have a job. For three hours per week I get to do something I like to do and actually get paid. Money! For me.

I shower and comb my hair and get dressed in nice clothes.

I get to be in the Avola log Schoolhouse with the lights and heat and books and people. Children come. I can help them choose books, or read to them aloud. Ladies come. I get to chat and laugh and hear the news. Teenagers come. I get to read their homework and make suggestions or help them do research. Older people come. To pass the time we do a puzzle and they tell their stories. It's like a dream come true!

But. There is a price to pay.

Elise and Michael, who are ten and nearly nine are allowed to come with me. But, as I get ready to make an exit, the younger children realize I am leaving. Nicholas and Toby are three and two years old. No matter what strategy I try, they start to cry. I have the supper ready. Kevin is willing to do the bedtime routine. But, still, tears, clinging, weeping, angry shouting. OK, the kids are so young. It's a normal reaction when the Mom goes away. But still, it sure takes the fun out of it. And, I feel mad at myself and guilty and doubt myself and wonder if I am permanently damaging my darling children in exchange for these three measly hours of adult life?

↘↓↙

I have absolutely no idea what to do differently? To take care of them or to take care of me.

I don't smoke or drink alcohol. I am not addicted to caffeine. I eat little sugar, well, except jam on my toast. We have tons of organic produce from our garden in the freezer and root cellar. I eat meat and other nutrients. What could I possibly do to improve my nutrition?

I don't exactly 'exercise' but, running after four kids, filling the wood box, shovelling the snow in winter and gardening in summer are all keeping me a normal weight.

I don't have a driver's license, so I can't do anything more except walking. I do walk. I go to the schoolhouse on Tuesdays to work at the library. I tutor a high school student on Wednesdays. I walk to the post office a couple of times a week.

I don't exactly have friends here. Cheryl moved away. Fran moved away. Debbie moved way. Opal moved away.

I phoned Cheryl. She said, "Go outside in Nature. Breathe in. Admire the beauty. Notice the birds."

I thought to myself, "No way! The entire world of 'Nature' is nothing but bleak, empty, monotone, overcast, dreary grey. I refuse to go outside."

Kevin said, "Maybe get out your guitar?"

I thought to myself, "No way! Singing makes me even more lonely. I miss Lori! I miss Liz! I miss being in the choir! I miss church! I miss my Mother playing the piano! Besides, cheerful songs make me feel worse. And sad songs are like poison. Even classical music like Daddy used to play on the record player just makes me homesick."

Saturday, February 16, 1991

I talked to my Mother on the phone. She said, "Read the Bible."

I thought to myself, "No way! First of all, it's too hard. Second of all, people fight about what it means. I get so confused. Third of all, I just get another wave of feeling homesick... but, how can I be homesick for the Seer-Church I left on purpose?"

I don't do preschool or Sunday School anymore. The little kids grew up. When the school closed so many families moved away. Besides, I have to focus on homeschooling every day.

I enjoy homeschooling so much in the autumn. I can envision the year, the curriculum and the materials I need to collect. I observe the children's interests. I make a habit of visiting the library and resource centre in Clearwater at the elementary school. But this midwinter slump is kind of scary. I have a huge responsibility to continue teaching our children and I cannot shirk this, whine, complain or resort to self-pity.

"While I get the supper ready, you can go take a nap," my husband sometimes suggests.

But I know I will lay there, listing problems and worries and composing lengthy tirades at myself for being lazy and sloth-like and fat and stupid. I lay awake at night and can't stay awake all day.

Magazines say, "Pamper yourself. Run a hot bubble bath. Light candles. Play soft music."

But, I can hear the children quarrelling, or getting into mischief, or watching TV shows they aren't allowed.

"Meditation," some say. "Be alone. Sit quietly. Light a candle. Empty your mind. Play a cassette tape. 'You are loved' the narrator drones."

I think to myself, "No way! Nobody loves me. I yell at the kids and disappoint my husband. I have no friends, my family never contacts me. I might phone someone, but they never phone me back. If I 'sit alone in the quiet,' my mind zooms with drudgery and muck and I conjure up proof that life is boring and dull and nothing I do matters."

I flip through magazines. I see perfect interior decorating, cheerful faces, slim women, splendid meals. Ugh. Nothing like that here. I switch on the TV. Lovely hair. Energetic young women. Capable, career, confident women smile out at me. Disgusting. How unrealistic!

Wallowing in self-doubt, self-pity, self-flagellation, I curl up in a cocoon. Where can I find a life raft? What thought can I hold one to? What can I do to change this darkness into some amount of light? There has to be something. Nobody can stay like this forever.

↘↓↙

Today I managed to cook a special dinner. Very close together, every February, we celebrate Valentine's Day, and also the anniversary of the day that Kevin and I met. Then comes Kevin's birthday and Michael's birthday. I roast a chicken golden brown with savoury herbs, creamed corn, green beans, carrot salad, and, yes, a chocolate cake. The children help make the table pretty with homemade cards for their Daddy's birthday and a calendar they have been working on as a homeschooling project. Everyone is smiling.

"It smells so good!" Kevin comments.

We say the blessing and just as I begin to serve the food, the phone rings. Kevin is called out to attend an accident on the highway. Leaving our family and his birthday feast, he volunteers to go out to provide first aid at the emergency situation.

We continue with the meal, but wait for him to return for the cake. However, inside, silently, the tension I feel is hard to hide from the children. Is the highway glare ice? Has a truck spilled hazardous, flammable, or poisonous material? Will the traffic pass safely, or will lookie-loos add to the commotion? How many people are injured? How seriously? How long will Kevin attend the scene alone? The ambulance and police have to drive for nearly an hour to arrive.

Most importantly: Will my husband come home safe?

His volunteer work is so different from my own. He is proud of my accomplishments. I am proud of his. He would never ask me to stop my involvement with the children. I would never ask him to stop the effective service he provides whenever he is called upon. We are both having an influence on history as we participate in our voluntary, Sacred Service.

But, oh, my heart is pounding! My ears are straining to hear the truck returning. My arms are hungry for his hug. My eyes are longing to see his face.

↘↓↙

The children are in bed. My husband is safely home. He has to leave for his night patrol in three hours. I've wrapped up a chicken sandwich and a piece of cake.

↘↓↙

What Happened Next for Kevin?

Kevin became an expert. First Aide. Ham Radio. Search and Rescue. Tracking. Highway Rescue.

He was often the first on-site at highway accidents providing care to the injured, and stayed until the RCMP, Coroner and Traffic Analyst completed their reports.

He has been called out for searches for snowmobilers, hunters, hikers, children, the elderly and river searches.

He continued with ongoing training. Later he became an instructor.

Meanwhile, on the railroad, he participated in the cleanup of derailments, fire, flood, avalanche and rock slides.

September, 2014, at a banquet attended by government officials and the entire Search and Rescue team, Kevin was presented with a framed certificate from the RCMP in appreciation of his 30 years of service as a Search and Rescue Volunteer.

↘↓↙

What Happened Next for Eleanor?

1993
After a family emergency sent me into panic mode, I realized I needed to go to counselling. What a relief to be able to unpack all of my questions, find resources to read, keep a journal, educate myself, express myself, nourish myself.[9]

The next February, when the doldrums loomed near, I was better prepared.

1994
What was it my counsellor said? I went to his lecture about depression and the bi-polar condition. He explained mental health as a physical need, not as a proof of strong willpower, or lack of character qualities. He explained that our brains make and need certain chemicals. One cell makes it, the other cell needs it. Some chemicals make the brain feel 'all is well.' Not having enough of that chemical makes the brain feel 'something is wrong' and may result in worry and fears that are hard to calm down. Not having enough may result in depression and dreary, grey, drab feelings, although there is nothing specific that is actually 'wrong.'

Saturday, February 16, 1991

I am 36 years old. I see on a chart of statistics that I am in an age group of many women with depression. Hormones may be starting to shift towards menopause. I have certainly had enough years of sleep deprivation to account for some imbalance within my brain chemistry. Stress about money and marriage and raising a family are always present.

The counsellor handed out a list of things that might help the brain make more of the chemicals needed to feel 'all is well.' Some things I can deliberately improve are: exercise, sunlight, hobbies, friends and things that make me smile, music to make my ears happy, art and patterns to make my eyes happy.

I kind of knew this already.

Since that first dreadful winter in 1978-79, I have stashed beautiful fabric and many colours of embroidery floss, colourful books and favourite quotes. But, crafts make such a mess... When will I ever have the energy to put everything away? I'll just be mad at myself all over again.

Music? I have plenty of cassette tapes of music I like. It just seems like a huge effort to get things set up. Plus, it almost feels like the songs are making fun of me, like a mean girl at school making fun of my clothing or my lunch box or my glasses. I can't be in a choir. I can't be in a band. I can't go to a church. I can't go to a concert. There is no pleasure in music alone.

It's easy to do good things for other people when I am volunteering, or for my husband, and for the children, or for my unborn baby when I am pregnant. But, when I try to take better care of myself, I have to struggle against this nasty sneering inside. Why is it so hard?

O, Dear, here we go again. Every path seems to lead to a dead end.

I am lost in a labyrinth. There is no way out. This is it. I am stuck.

I have no energy for housework. Besides the effort, housework is also a lot of problem solving. What shall I do with this this lone sock? Where shall I put this unanswered letter?

I seem to have two speeds. Nothing and Mad. I yell at the kids to come do their chores. I slam the pots and pans around to get the kitchen straight. I slop through the dishes, barking orders to the children to sweep, move the laundry around, feed the dog, straighten the boots.

Dirty laundry is heaped up. Overflowing baskets of clean laundry are lined up beside my bed. Papers and clutter spill across every horizontal surface. It is entirely overwhelming... even on a good day.

"I wish I was someplace else," I moan into my pillow.

In a moment of clarity I realize, "I am here."

It is midwinter. Every plant and animal knows this. They have either migrated, hibernated, or stored food for the months of snow covered mountains. The trees and plants have become dormant, storing their sap in their roots, waiting, waiting. They know that sunshine and warmth will return. Insects have either laid eggs to continue the life cycle in the springtime, or are waiting in a semi-alive larvae stage, believing that a new day will dawn.

I cannot migrate. I cannot hibernate. I do have stored food.

Maybe, I am like a squirrel. I will have active days and stay-in-the-nest days. Gladly, I did not die when I brought forth a new generation. I can stay and parent them for many years to come.

Maybe, like the trees and wildflowers, I can accept the fact that dormancy is part of life. Not every day is a happy-skipping-through-the-daisies day. Some of the life cycle is simply: Waiting.

Maybe, if I am not so harsh with myself, expecting productivity and 'do my best' every single day of the year, I can simply:

Saturday, February 16, 1991

rest, read a book, dabble, tinker, mosey and not put so much pressure on myself.

Maybe, I can recognize that, "This is where I am in the cycle." Maybe I will be able to just 'be' there and not struggle against the forces of Nature. Morning, noon, evening, night. Yes, that is a real cycle. Spring, summer, fall, winter. Yes, that is a real cycle. Infancy, childhood, youth, productive adult, older adult. Yes, that is also a real cycle. Not to mention a woman's monthly cycle, weaving hormones and energy into every part of the month, and perhaps the beginning of my own body changing from childbearing years to dormancy inside my ovaries and womb. Maybe there is a daily, an annual and a life cycle I can be aware of and appreciate. There are predictable patterns in Nature.

Maybe, I can move with the cycle and not push against it.

↘↓↙

I bring the kettle to a boil and brew chamomile tea. I compliment Kevin as he helps me make supper and indicate to the children that they need to get ready for bed. I take my Journal and try to find words to preserve the realization I have come to.

You wouldn't plant flowers in the wintertime. Baby birds and animals would never live. Butterflies cannot tolerate the cold. The vegetable garden needs light that is simply not available at this time of year at this latitude. Yet, they each survive. They do not try to outsmart the winter. They adapt. How do people adapt in Northern Climates?

Now my mind zooms around the globe, collecting images I have seen of other civilizations. The Norse tell tall tales of heroes, victories, gods and goddesses. The Laplanders and Polish embroider wide borders of colour across their clothing. Danes have a custom, called 'Hygge' which is a kind of nesting that takes them through these long months of indoor living. Inuit have games and challenges which sharpen their skills, build community spirit, keep the muscles trim, and encourage family cheerfulness. European cultures have long stories and ballads, complex musical compositions, poetry and theatre, painting and sculpture as well as science and medical discoveries. All of these would not be available if these people were nomads, hunting and travelling. These cultures have all developed because people have for centuries spent so many indoor hours at the fireside.

I may not be able to cheer myself up entirely with these thoughts, but I can become better oriented to the reality I am living in.

It is helpful to realize that I am not alone.

Chapter 5
Monday, March 6, 1995

What need we teach a child
with our books and rules?
Let him walk among the hills and flowers,
let him gaze upon the waters,
let him look up at the stars
and he will have his wisdom.
  —Author Unknown

↖↑↗

"Mom! It's crusty snow!" Nicholas, nearly eight years old, has rosy cheeks from his chilly trip out to the chicken barn this morning.

"Mom! Can we go?" Toby, now six-and-a-half, has such an eager face, waiting for me to agree. Since Elise and Michael go to high school now, and Kevin works on the railroad during the day, we three have the day to ourselves.

Crusty snow is rare and only lasts for a short time, a few days of each winter, a few hours of each day. Warm days, or rain, make the top layer of snow melt. Then, the cold nights turn that soft, wet snow to a thick layer of ice. In the early morning, it is possible to walk on top of the snow. We welcome the freedom to wander where ever we want to after walking on only the road or the path for the previous four months. It is important to take action right away if we want to enjoy the experience. If the sun comes out, by afternoon, the snow will melt again and then we will unexpectedly break through the crust and wallow in the deep. Or rain might return and the snow will become mushy slush. After a few days of the temperature going back and forth between thawing and freezing, the whole structure disintegrates like a bowl of crystallized particles.

Up on the mountains, crusty snow may become hazardous. Deep new snow might fall on top of the icy crust, pressing the weight down, creating a slab layer which could release an avalanche.

But for us, it is an extra-special day. And one I look forward to every year.

Nicholas and Toby are homeschooling. After lessons, their days might include explorations, building forts, dragging brush for a bonfire or searching for bird's nests. In the years we've lived here, beside the river, I have learned to celebrate the tiniest changes and call them 'Spring.' In March, I hear the honking of Canada geese returning, and notice that the birds and squirrels are getting 'twitter-pated.' Soon the Spring Equinox will bring daylight that is longer than darkness. Easter cards, toys and colours are in the stores. We are almost done with winter!

I scan the day's plans, look at the eager faces and nod, "Yes!" But with a condition. "First we have to have breakfast, and I'll plan supper, so let's be quick! The sun will be up in an hour and the snow will probably be soft by one o'clock."

"Let's pack a picnic!" Toby suggests.

"I'll get my backpack," Nicholas offers.

"Mom, can we ski?" Toby always adds to the adventure. Grampa Hinkle made an order from the Sears catalogue at Christmastime and outfitted the children with cross-country skis.

"Yes. No. Wait." I am thinking fast. "Let's not take the skis this time. We have done that before. Let's hike. Let's explore the swamp!"

After so many years with a diaper bag, infant carrier, naps, cautioning the older ones to wait for the younger ones, at last, we can step out and take a full advantage of this spectacular day!

"Wear layers," I remind them. "We start out chilly, but soon we'll be warm." T-shirt, sweater, coat, snow pants, boots, hat, scarf, mittens, and we each pack a water bottle and lunch in our backpacks. I slide the little camera into my pocket. There are six pictures left on this roll of film.

↖↑↗

We set out into the forest. Our trusty black lab, Jasper, bounds and yelps, enthusiastically. Even he is tired of walking only on the road or path. Now he can sniff and run and explore and zig-zag all over the place.

Three explorers and our pup, we cut across the smooth, white lawn, walking about a meter above the garden, past the crab-apple tree, the lone oak tree, beside the huge spruce and past the chicken barn. We leave behind the scraggly blackberry rows and corn stalks poking up through the snow. Down, down below, I know that the rhubarb is secretly beginning to nudge up through the soil towards the sun. Onions, potatoes and garlic left in the garden through the winter can also sense signs of spring.

Now we trudge beside the river, up on the snowbanks.

Sometimes we have to wait for three days for the snowplow to come down our road. Sometimes there is a light snow and we can use the cross-country skis on the roadway. Sometimes the plow truck does not drop sand. Then the thaw and freeze during several days and nights eventually builds up a smooth layer of ice and we can skate up and down the length of our whole road. But today we don't have limitations. It is such a relief to not have to walk on the road, or shovel the paths. The dog is bounding. The boys are climbing up the high snowbanks. We all feel the excitement.

Careful while we cross the train tracks, we climb a gentle slope, push through the undergrowth and find the place we are looking for. There is a clear right-of-way which follows an oil pipeline. We have come here to ski in previous years. The crusty snow makes the smooth slope very fast. With such a wide age-range between the children, we have never gone farther, but stay and repeat the skiing on the same slope for the day.

However, the two older ones are away for the school day, and these younger two are not little kids anymore. They will have the stamina to take a longer hike than we have ever attempted before.

"Tell me where we are. How would you get home?" I pause to make sure the boys are oriented and paying attention.

"We're kind of in a box," Nicholas notices. "The train tracks and river are on that side, the road to the cemetery is on the other side. The highway is behind us and the swamp is in front of us."

There is no danger of getting lost.

Monday, March 6, 1995

It's too early for bears to be out. No hunters or tourists. No logging in the area. We are in the wilderness, but not in any danger.

At the base of the hill, the swampy land reaches all the way to the river. In the summertime mosquitoes swarm. The water is not deep, but is too mucky for wading. The brush and humps of fallen trees interrupt the ice so there is no chance of skating. Now, with the security of exceptionally hard crusty snow, we are in no danger of breaking through.

Smooth, brown velvet cattails burst apart with a zillion seeds when the boys sword fight. Willow twigs swell with soon-to-open pussy willows. What are these tall straight twigs that blush a deep red? Cottonwood buds will soon share their scent. Here is a short tree with long thorns. I don't remember seeing that one before. Somewhere nearby, there are Saskatoon bushes. I have seen their white flowers in May. Skunk cabbage, ferns, and other water plants are buried under winter's blanket.

Yellowy-green birch catkins are just beginning to dangle down. Kevin taught the boys how to collect the sap from birch trees. They recently drilled holes in the trees on our land, then hammered in a little pipe to drain the sap into buckets. Much like maple sap, this clear liquid can be slowly simmered to become a thick, sweet syrup.

"Mom! Look!" Toby has gone ahead and made a discovery. "What do you think made this?" There is a wide place where the snow is all broken in and trampled down. Toby shows me where deep tracks have pierced the snow. I see the tips of all the twigs have been nibbled off, showing the green sappy inside under the grey bark.

"I think a moose had lunch here!" I suggest.

"I see rabbit tracks," Nicholas observes. "Looks like they go back and forth here a lot."

"If I were a coyote, I'd love crusty snow for hunting," Toby imagines.

Indeed, crusty snow is also to the wolves' advantage. In the same way that our dog can run on top of the snow, the wolves' wide paws are suited for them to hunt. Moose and deer break through the crust with their hooves and make easy prey.

"Did you hear the coyotes calling last night?" I ask. "They are calling for their mates at this time of year. They can cross the river and gather together. Their pups will be born by the time it is warmer. Most animals have their young in the springtime."

During our homeschooling lessons, we have already talked about the names of the baby animals. The mule deer fawns, moose calves, bear cubs, cougar kittens, wolf and coyote pups will be born. Chicks, tadpoles, fingerlings and all kinds of insects will hatch. On the farm, lambs, calves, piglets and colts will soon be born.

Somehow, every species knows what time it is. Hibernating, migrating or staying, they know where to go and what to eat, how to find a mate and where to build a nest.

"I wonder what other signs of wildlife we can find?" I encourage the boys to look around as we hike. We have no destination, but wander here and there as the openings between the brush allows.

Almost at the same time, in opposite directions, both boys call out, "I see a nest!" Sure enough, with the high snow, it is easy to reach into the bush and break away the twigs to release each nest. One is solid and heavy, lined with mud and very sturdy. The other one is twigs woven and kind of loosely fit together. I brought a bag to collect things, and carefully wrap them before we go on. Now that they have had success, it seems there are nests all through the lowlands. One is a tiny, soft, round collection of black fibres. Another is mostly grass.

I wish I knew what kind of bird made each one. It is so amazing to hold these ingenious constructions in our hands.

We find a long fallen log and set out our picnic things. What a beautiful day. The foggy morning has cleared into a bright blue sky. We will have to head back to the road before we start to break through the crust. But, not yet.

This season in-between winter and spring is one of my favourite times of the year. It is not bitter cold, but there is still snow. The daylight comes earlier, but there is no mud yet. Changes are coming.

To make a little more homeschooling in this day, I prompt the boys to consider a few things.

"Did you notice the fence posts over there?" I begin to take their thinking in a new direction. "The family who built our house also worked on this part of the land. They dug ditches to drain the lowlands and grew hay crops for their animals. If they had enough hay, they could sell some. Let's think about the ways their family lived in their time, and we live in our time, and how we are the same and how we are different."

"We both have a woodshed," Nicholas begins, "So they would be watching their pile of wood get smaller by this time of year, too."

"Good. What else are we starting to run out of by this time of year?" I continue.

"The root cellar," Toby answers.

"Yes, I have to keep track of what we have the most of and use it up, what we're running out of and what might be going bad," I explain.

"I saw some potatoes sprouting so we can plant them again," Nicholas knows.

"So, we don't want to use up everything. If we eat it all now, we will be hungry later," Toby has noticed an ancient problem in agricultural civilizations and has realized its solution.

"Did the other family have electricity?" Toby wonders.

"Not at first. Electricity came to Avola in the early 1970s. People had kerosene lamps, wood stoves, heated up water in big pots, and had no electricity." I fill in the information they are asking for.

"Like you and Daddy had when you lived in the cabin?" Nicholas likes to put two and two together.

"So, they didn't have telephone, or TV, or a video machine, or a computer, either?" Toby realizes.

"But, it gets dark so early. I wonder what they did in the evening?" Both boys try to imagine.

"I don't know for sure, but we could ask one of the Old Timers when we schedule another interview," I suggest. "But, I'll bet that when they were kids, they played the same way you do when springtime comes." Jump rope, hop scotch, ball games, flying kites, bows and arrows, smashing rocks through the ice, stomping in puddles, building dams in the water trickling down the road. These and other childhood activities in the early spring are nearly identical then and now. "And, I'll bet the mothers in both times scolded their kids, 'You're tramping mud all over the floor!' just the same way I do when we do the spring cleaning."

Lunch is over. We pack up and decide which direction to explore next.

"Can we go to the beaver pond?" Toby asks. In the summertime we have found lots of stumps left where their teeth have cut and felled saplings. There are lots of beaver-sticks with the bark chewed off. Over on the far bank, there is a muddy mound of sticks they built for their lodge. Once, when the pond was low, we could see their waterways and where they gathered the nutrient rich branches to store for the winter.

Monday, March 6, 1995

ᚴ↑ᚵ

I remember an excellent homeschooling day we had when another family came to visit. We made a big tent in the living room with tables, chairs, sheets and blankets. The children collected pillows and quilts, books and stuffed toys.

I was happy that seven children were cooperating. I thought of an idea to make it last longer. "Is this your beaver lodge?" While they decided who was the Mom and Dad and children beavers, made an entryway and coordinated who would be on lookout, I went to the kitchen to prepare long, thin things for them to eat. I cut carrot sticks and long cheese slices. I already had bread dough rising, so I rolled out long sticks, salted them and baked them for the beavers to chew on. The dog became the dangerous hunter.

"Beavers are nocturnal." I encouraged them to stay quiet and cozy while I found a few more educational activities. I opened the encyclopedia and showed them the beaver lodge interior. I gave them Canadian nickles with the beaver on one side, paper and crayons so they could make rubbings. I crawled inside as the 'grandmother beaver' to explain the way beavers benefit other animals. "It's amazing to consider how many generations live in the same place, build dams, and change the landscape. Damming a creek, filling a swamp, slowing the water means that silt collects and new kinds of plants grow which are food for insects, fish, birds and animals. Safe places are created and waterfowl raise their young." And I gave them a quick peek into how Canadian history was shaped by the beavers when trappers moving ever westward, guided by the First Nations Peoples, searched for more beaver pelts, built trading posts and forts, and mapped their routes.

March Chapter 5

↖↑↗

We have to cross a snow-bridge to get to the beaver pond. The sun has been shining for awhile, so we have to test the crust. First, the dog crosses, then Toby, then Nicholas. I go last. Oops! I get a soaker. But, we will soon be home. And, it is worth a little chill to see and hear what we found. Ripples of water are bubbling under thin, clear ice. The patterns and gurgles are ever-changing, in contrast to the silent, un-moving whiteness of the rest of the landscape.

The sun will go behind the wall-like mountain by 2:00pm, so we head for home. We all have rosy cheeks and there's time for some cocoa. Kevin will be home by 4:00. The high school bus will bring Elise and Michael home at 4:30.

I get a big pot of spaghetti started. The two homeschoolers take time to do a little bit of writing about the outing. Kevin is safely home. Elise and Michael trudge down the hill from the school bus stop. Soon darkness closes the day.

↖↑↗

While we are all at the table, each family member reports on their day.

We continue learning from our adventure by asking Kevin about this season for various workers.

On the railroad and highway, the hazards of cold, dark, snow and ice are receding. Now flooding, mud slides and falling trees challenge the people who work outside all year. Crews watch for places where a tiny crack might fill with water during the daytime, freeze at night, expand and sheer rocks off to block transportation corridors.

The season for trapping comes to an end. The thick winter coats of the valuable fur-bearing animals will shed and it is time for each kind of animal to pair off to raise young. The marten, mink, otter, beaver and coyote pelts collected during the winter are prepared to sell.

Logging comes to a halt during 'break-up.' Mud prevents the heavy equipment from safely climbing the mountain roads.

In the days before electricity, homesteaders hauled blocks of ice and packed them with layers of sawdust so they would to be able to store food all summer.

"Dad, when it's your weekend, if it's still crusty snow, can you take us to Pin Cherry Island?" Toby hasn't had enough exploring. We went there by canoe once. It's just a little upriver from where we live. In the springtime, the river is moving too fast. But, in low water, in the autumn, the large sandbar around the island was fun to explore. I like to bring home driftwood. Kevin found signs of an old cabin. The teenagers had fun climbing on a huge log with big twisted roots. We could walk all the way around the tiny island. There was no hazard of deep water or getting lost.

"That was so fun to go dog sledding." Michael remembers an outing years ago when Kevin's friend, Brent, brought his dog team and we zoomed out into the meadow near Pin Cherry Island. "It was before you were born," he explains to the younger brothers. "I always wondered if the dogs were forced to pull, but they loved it. They were so excited to get harnessed up and run!"

"I liked going barefoot in the sunshine," Elise recalls a summertime outing, "and picking the bright red pin cherries for jelly."

Good memories.

↖↑↗

No one really needs me to put them to bed anymore, but Nicholas makes an irresistible request. "Tell me a story about your life."

"I will tell you about the outings that my Mother and Daddy took my brothers and sisters on. Someday I hope to take you to these places, too." And I describe what I remember about the Empire State Building, the Statue of Liberty, the Grand Canyon, standing at the top of Pikes Peak, feeding rye crackers to the giraffes at the zoo. I marched with the Girl Scouts in a parade, saw the musical 'Kismet' on stage, lined up at the movie theatre for 'The Sound of Music.' We all took a ride on a glass bottomed boat, went swimming in the ocean, collected sea shells in Florida. In Canada we went to the Farmer's Market, Montreal, Ottawa, Niagara Falls, Oktoberfest. Later I was in a marching band. And of course our family went to church, sport events, swimming, skating, camping, and to visit grandparents and cousins.

As I return down the stairs, I preserve this day in my permanent memory. I never want to forget this Crusty Snow Hike with these two curious sons.

My parents have told me of their childhood outings to swim, and climb, and visit farms, and museums. They took me on outings. Now I take my children on outings. Someday will my children take their children on outings?

↖↑↗

What Happened Next?
The years sped by. The children left home. This particular 'Crusty Snow' day was preserved in my memory so clearly that

it became the inspiration for one of my 'Valley Voices' newspaper articles for the North Thompson Times.[10]

Like Laura Ingalls Wilder, I was beginning to write my memoir by composing short stories for the newspaper.

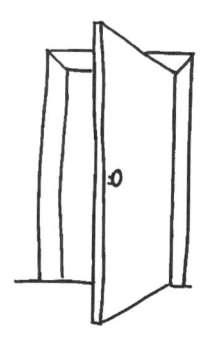

Chapter 6
this year 'February' lasts from Christmas Eve, 1996... until May, 1997... a total of 139 days

> That terrible mood of depression
> of whether it's any good or not
> is known as 'The Artist's Reward.'
> —*Ernest Hemmingway*

↘↓↙

Some people say 'Live in the Moment...' For me, there is no 'moment.' There is only boredom and emptiness and repetition.
   Without the Past I have no foundation or purpose.
   Without the Future I have no direction or goal.
   If I cut myself off from the Past I have no root.

If I trim away the Future I am rudderless and adrift on a vast empty sea.

If I 'stay in the Present?' Now? There is only a trackless, snowy desert. Wandering. Fog. No compass. No map. Nothing to orient myself to. I cannot find my bearings.

Some people say 'Follow your heart.'

No. Without my head, I have no words, only feelings. My Counsellor taught me there are four feelings (and a zillion variations). Mad. Sad. Glad. Afraid.

If I only have feelings then I sink down into the mire. Feeling sorry for myself. Misery. Tears. Storm. Lost in the sadness of being so alone.

No. I do not allow myself to enter the corridor marked 'Sad.' There are too many friends who's voices I cannot hear, faces and smiles I cannot see, connections broken. No interactions. No one is glad to see my face.

No. I cannot enter the corridor marked 'Mad.' It is way too scary to vent, or froth, or roar, or whine. How will I find my way back to sensible, balanced and wholesome? No. I do not want to make room for these feelings.

No. I will not enter the corridor marked 'Afraid.' Fear seems everywhere. Slippery snow, bitter cold, no transportation, frightening injury, dangerous fire. If I allowed myself to acknowledge it, I would realize that I am afraid of everything all of the time. When my husband is away, I am home alone with four children. How could I possibly manage an emergency? And, more significant than a physical threat, I am also afraid of the impact I am having on the children. If I do correct them... if I do not. If I shout, spank, 'go to your room,' or 'time out,' how do I know I am 'doing the right thing?' But, if I turn the other way, don't see the misdeed, let it go unchecked, what then? Maybe a lie told to me now will grow into defrauding the government? Maybe sibling rivalry will become gang violence? Maybe snitching a cookie will become a drug addiction? Maybe 'potty mouth' will become lack of respect for all authority? Maybe a push, or a pinch, or a slap will become domestic abuse? How shall I govern? Punish? Lecture? 'It's just a phase they go through' or 'Boys will be boys.'

I am a Mother. No matter how my kids 'turn out,' I am 'damned if I do and damned if I don't.'

That leaves the corridor of emotion marked 'Glad.' Really? Can I deliberately stay cheerful? What is there to look forward to? What do my eyes see or ears hear that is pleasant? How can I obtain pleasant music? What memories of people, places, faces, beauty or art can I savour in my mind to create a bridge from this monochromatic world, to believing that colour and creative beauty exists? Surely this dark forest of snow-laden, bowing branches is not the only thing in existence?

Glad? Yes. I am glad for the Past. Glad for the Future. In the Present, I must keep the water out of my canoe in order to stay afloat, not allow the weight to drag me down, keep my mind above my heart, deliberately shushing the anxiety, deliberately choosing 'Yes' when 'No' is so obvious.

↘↓↙

Last year, in January, 1996, my Daddy died.[11]

When there's a death in the family, people turn to their religious beliefs. What happens after we die?

I realized that the most valuable inheritance that my Dad gave my siblings and I, was his dedication to the Seer-Church.[12] Although I deliberately left the Church Community, I decided to do my best to pass on the teachings while homeschooling our children. When they reached high school, Kevin and I had a big decision to make. Shall we send our children to the Bonnie Hills Church School in Pennsylvania? Founded on the

Seer-Church doctrines, it is where Daddy went to school, and later I did, and, as they each came to be the right age, all of my siblings did, too.

It seems like a golden opportunity. But, sending my children so far away made a pain inside me like nothing I have ever experienced. I felt like my heart was ripped from my chest.

Paperwork. Packing. Airport.

In late August, 1996, my firstborn child, my only daughter, my precious heart-song, Elise, left home to attend the Bonnie Hills Church School for Grade 11.

Daddy died. Elise left home. Both of these turning points have had a big impact on me this year. People I love, leave me.

My role as a Mother is shifting. No more babies. Time. Changes. The Empty Nest. Mortality.

'Live in the moment' doesn't seem solid. I need stability and continuity. Time seems to erase everything I have worked for. I need something that will endure.

↘↓↙

This year, the seasonal bout with midwinter-blues started at Christmas time, 1996, and I didn't take action until May, 1997. It was a very long 'February.'

↘↓↙

It had been the best Christmas ever.

I volunteered to participate in seven events and productions in two towns. I did well. I had an impact on children, families, and the elderly. I estimated 1000 people had seen the shows, heard the songs, been touched by the Christmas Baby, through my creativity and volunteering.

But, when the house was quiet on Christmas Eve, Scripture readings, poetry recitations and songs complete, notes to Santa tucked into the empty stockings, cookies and milk set just so, visions of sugar plums dancing in the children's heads, I paused for a peaceful, resting moment for myself.

Favourite nightgown (red and white polka dot flannel with little black Toto dogs), favourite tea (mint with a little honey), favourite mug (the one with the bald eagle soaring above the snow capped mountain peaks), favourite chair (the rocking chair my Mother and Daddy gave me when Elise was born), wrapped in my favourite afghan (Oma crocheted for our wedding gift), I pulled my chair beside the cozy fire, sat back to think over the last few weeks and be sure I was ready for Christmas morning.

And, with a sigh in the stillness, having carefully set the stage for a quiet, calm, celebration and satisfaction at my achievement, I was taken completely by surprise. The first thought that popped into my head was this: "Why was I ever born?"

Really? That is my mountain top declaration?

Again.

"Nothing I have ever have done actually matters."

I felt like I was struggling up from a too-deep dive underwater, scared, seeking oxygen, with a great effort to return to normalcy.

"Kevin," I quietly called my husband closer. "Please hug me. I don't feel so well."

Without raising my voice to draw the attention of my slumbering children, I described my out-of-proportion feeling of discouragement and also recounted the accomplishments I had recently achieved.

"How could I possibly be feeling this low? I have just had such a wonderful time preparing for Christmas this year?"

I listed off the successful events and productions I had participated in this December.

"First, was the party for the employee's children." It had been an unexpected bonus. One day in mid-November I asked to use the telephone in the office at the Clearwater grocery store. The staff were talking, trying to solve a problem. I overheard enough to ask, "You need entertainment for your staff Christmas party? What are you wishing for?" I offered to do it. They offered to pay me to prepare entertainment for a family-style party. I dressed as Mrs. Santa, with a long black velvet skirt, white blouse and red vest, red socks and hair tie. I powdered my hair and wore granny glasses. I made a puzzle, prepared a craft, brought my guitar, invented a memory game and taught the children a little folk dance. It was a huge bonus for our family to have an additional $70 to spend on Christmas goodies: cheese and crackers, olives and pickles, eggnog and marzipan, candy canes and tinsel.

"Second, was the homeschooling support group event." In early December, our family participated in a Wintertime-Christmastime event in Clearwater. We made a map on the classroom floor, built a scene with a town, roads, farm, forest, animals and river. We made up a story about ecology, and seasons, and cooperation. Plus, we had a splendid sing-along. I played my guitar accompanied by the children with rhythm instruments.

"Third, was my dance class." My students held a recital for their parents at Evergreen Acres so the seniors living in the residence could come. The youngest children improvised *A Snowflake Dance*, another group prepared the *March of the Toy Soldiers*. Also a scene of *The Nutcracker* was presented. Local piano teachers shared the accomplishments of their students. Four women in an acapella group made us laugh with a rendition of *T'was the Night Before Christmas* sung to the tune of *Chopsticks*.

"Fourth, was at the Avola Community Hall." The traditional Christmas Concert this year was inspired by 'Winnie the Pooh.' Each child dressed up as a toy animal. The toy animals wanted to give each other gifts. There were problems to solve, a song, a dance, and a happy ending.

"Fifth, and best of all, my friends at the Catholic church invited me to direct their children's Nativity play." The children rehearsed and preformed the shadow play so reverently. The audience enjoyed the way it was presented. The dinner and carol sing was so festive.

"Sixth, was at the elementary school." I taught the primary grades in Clearwater sign language for *Long Time Ago in Bethlehem*. The children learned to sing and sign at the same time. Cheryl told me that children up and down her street were teaching it to their siblings, parents and neighbours. The audience was spell bound. The whole school ended up learning this simple, yet heartwarming song and method of delivery. 360 students, each with two or more family members as guests, made a total of nearly 1000 people!

"I stayed home with the three boys while you drove to Seattle to pick up Elise from the airport. I was so glad she made it home for Christmas after her first semester at the Bonnie Hills Church high school." It was hard to wait anxiously without any way to communicate while they made their way over the midwinter mountain passes. Not until the headlights shone in the driveway could I know, at last, that they were safely home.

"So, tonight, was the seventh. When we were all together for our Christmas Eve candlelight service at home, my heart was so happy." With no church for miles in either direction, it has become such a satisfaction to hear the voices of my children and husband read aloud from Luke and Matthew and for me to prepare hymns on the guitar.

"Yes, all seven different, challenging, satisfying events." All ran smoothly. And, to top it off, I had meals, laundry, chores, homeschooling and Christmas customs for our own family all ready without any appearance of stressful pressure and yelling.

"So? Why would I feel anything except thankful relaxation now that my challenges have been met and accolades collected and everything in order for Christmas Day tomorrow?"

"Maybe you're tired," Kevin gently suggested.

"I don't feel tired. I just feel 'So what?' That's worse, I think." I was really puzzled. How could such a glad moment come instantly crashing down?

Kevin helped me tidy up the room and prepare the midnight Christmas Eve magic so we could get to bed at a reasonable hour.

But, I kept listening inside my mind for any return of that heavy, 'So what?' feeling.

↘↓↙

Day after day, I felt cold all the time. I just couldn't get warm. The wood stove fire, layers of woollen clothing, even curled up in bed didn't help.

Elise went back to Pennsylvania. Michael went on the school bus to high school in Clearwater. Nicholas and Toby had homeschool assignments.

I ended up calling the children to bring me their books and lessons. I gave instruction from my pillows. I invited them to bring decks of cards, puzzles, and of course the laundry to fold all on my bed.

I kept napping. For years I have been taking a nap with the little ones after lunch. Now I added a 10:00am nap while they did their lessons and watched their TV shows. In the afternoon, I was too tired to think of supper plans, so I went to lie down. After a simplified menu, Michael washed up and I went upstairs to read with the younger ones and fell asleep on their beds. If I woke up in the night, then I moved down to my own bed in the wee hours of the morning. But, I tossed and turned, worried and felt grumpy for the rest of the night.

The routines of winter kept things rolling. You have to get wood. You have to eat. You have to do laundry. You have to keep the cycle of family chores revolving. But I was always tired.

I was in the doldrums.

Meanwhile, I discovered that two of my friends had prescriptions for antidepressant medication.

Ella was a stay-at-home Mom living in less than ideal circumstances. She was practical and suggested, "Try it. You can always stop."

Laura was a professional woman with a major role in the community. She coached me gently, "What does it cost you, your husband, your children, and your own interests for you to be feeling low so much of every day?"

I asked them how they decided to take the medication? What effect it had? I was skeptical. I was cautious. I had never used drugs, alcohol, tobacco or even coffee.

Meanwhile, several of my friends phoned me at the strangest times of day. 9:00 in the morning. Noon, 2:00 in the afternoon. 4:00. 8:00... Didn't they know someone might be taking a nap?

Then I realized: I am in bed all of the time. I was hibernating. But, it was already the month of May!

February Chapter 6

↘↓↙

I phoned my friend, Laura. "Eleanor," her voice was warm, but firm. "I want you to hang up. Phone the doctor's office. Make an appointment. Then phone me back to tell me you did it."

I did.

I chose a lady doctor for the first time in my life, thinking she would be compassionate, thorough, listen and gently understand.

I asked for blood tests for iron and for thyroid. "What else can make you tired all the time?" But before the test results were back, she said, "I think you are depressed. I can prescribe medications."

My jaw dropped open. I was stunned. A wave of fear crashed over me. This is it! The dreaded mental health moment! I was terrified! I practically ran out of the examining room and straight for the telephone. I could hardly see straight as I dialed the number and insisted I speak with the counsellor.

"I need to see you now! Right now. Today. Please!"

I took his lunch hour. I was so scared. He gave me a video tape to watch at home. Elizabeth Manley was the narrator. She was a well-known Canadian figure skater, the silver medallist in the 1988 Calgary Olympics. She explained what it felt like to be in clinical depression. A scientist showed a diagram and description of the cells, the chemistry lacking and the way the medication worked.

For the next few days I tried to comprehend it all with my mind. I phoned my Mother, "Did you ever take antidepressants?"

"No. I focused on what I could do. I was very self-disciplined. Besides, the only things available on the 1970s were drugs I did not want to have in my body. Also, it would not have fixed the problems I was having. I wanted to solve them myself."

But, then I wondered. Would their marriage have survived if she had taken the medication? Will mine survive if I don't?

"Some of my sisters have experienced depression," she continued, "And there is a strong thread of it in your Dad's family tree."

That was both reassuring and ominous information.

↘↓↙

At about that same time, Kevin's Mom was experiencing some hearing loss, but she refused to use a hearing aid. I wondered how much she was missing in family gatherings, playing cards with her friends and other social activities. Then we heard that she had narrowly escaped being hit by a bus! A bystander pulled her back as she stepped off the sidewalk to cross the street. She hadn't heard it coming!

"Kevin, I want to tell you what I think. If I needed a hearing aid, that would not be anything to be ashamed of. I already wear glasses. Your Dad needed insulin. Some people take enzymes to aid in their digestion. It seems to me, from the information on this video, that there are cells in the brain that make a chemical called 'serotonin' and other cells that need it. When a person is experiencing clinical depression, it is because either the cells that make it are not making enough, or the cells that want it are not getting enough. The medication simply restores the ratio and the brain gets what it needs. It doesn't sound so scary when I understand what is happening and how the correction is made. It is a physical lack with a physical solution." My mind was shifting from fear to logic. Information was the key.

"Kevin, what do you think? If I had one leg shorter then the other, and it strained my back, so it hurt, so I yelled at everybody because my back hurt, but I did not want to use an elevated shoe, that would be silly. Sure, people will see the shoe, but I won't hurt all the time, or be yelling at everyone." Now I was struggling with the 'What will they think of me?' social stigma of admitting that I had a difficulty classified as 'Mental Health.'

I got a prescription for the smallest dose. The doctor and pharmacist explained that it would take six weeks to be effective, but I noticed an improvement in three days!

↘↓↙

It felt so good to feel good.

I didn't have to be super busy, or mad, or exhausted, or grumpy. I could just have a 'normal' day. A little housework. Focus on homeschooling for a few hours. Tinker in the garden. Make some supper.

Easy enough to do.

It was such a relief to feel better. I could sleep at night. I stayed awake in the day. I wasn't simmering with anger towards myself, my husband, my kids. I wasn't feeling sorry for myself all the time. I wasn't worried, inventing hypothetical hazards.

I vowed never to allow myself to get so low again.

↘↓↙

Three times it happened that I went away from home for a few days and forgot to take the capsules with me. 'Poor me' came back. And 'Who cares.' My gloomy self-talk returned. The tasks for the day seemed overwhelming. Mountains of laundry. Infinity of dishes. Warehouses overflowing with shoes and boots. Clutter in the hallway. Avalanches of paper on every table. Everything my husband said, or did, or didn't say, or didn't do was irritating.

I had accidentally set up a test to see if the medication was effective. Clearly, there were benefits. I continued with regularity.

↘↓↙

What Happened Next?
"May I cut back? Reduce the dose? Use the medication seasonally? Maybe I don't need it anymore?" These questions came up with various doctors over several years. I cut back gradually until I was sure that none was needed.

But, I also promised myself to recognize the gloomy thoughts and heavy sensations and address the problem immediately if it ever returned.

1996-2003
Elise and Michael both left home to attend, first high school, and then college at the Church Community in Pennsylvania.

2004
Nicholas and Toby left in the autumn to go to the Church School, too.

I had self-employment and travel plans in place to keep me focused.

Michael was getting married! Kevin and I planned to attend the ceremony in Pennsylvania in October. Because Cheryl had attended his birth, I invited her to come to the wedding as our guest.

Added to that, Cheryl and I planned a 30-day train trip across the USA. We had a complex and highly successful adventure.

November went by.

Nicholas and Toby came home for Christmas. Kevin and I enjoyed listening to them tell of their experiences. We made our traditional gingerbread cut-out cookies, decorated the tree and went skating on the mill pond.

2005

After the holidays, Kevin drove the boys over the mountains, across the border, back to the Seattle airport.

And then it came. I dreaded it. The Empty Nest.

Clunk. I took a real downturn.

At first I thought I was just resting. After all, I had spent a lot of energy. At first I thought I was just cozy. It was so nice to watch TV all day. No diapers. No homeschooling. No schedule. Kevin was at work in the daytime now so I was home alone.

When Kevin left for work at 6:00am, I could watch 'Quincy.' After I ate breakfast and got the kitchen put back together, the next show was 'Red Green,' then 'Oprah,' followed by 'Dr. Oz.' All afternoon there were talk shows and we also got a movie channel. On different weeknights there were reruns of 'Cosby Show,' 'Touched by and Angel,' 'Road to Avonlea,' 'Little House on the Prairie,' 'Matlock,' 'Columbo,' 'Murder She Wrote,' and 'The Waltons.'

If nothing was on, I would just roll over on the couch and take a nap.

One day, I had to admit, I felt that heavy, dreary, 'Why was I ever born?' feeling.

I made a doctor's appointment in Clearwater. But, I couldn't get there! That was the day that the highway bridge washed out! Bitter cold had locked a swift river tributary with unusually thick ice. Suddenly, a warmer temperature brought heavy rain. The river rose, lifting slabs of ice the size of a grand piano, which smashed against the concrete supports holding up the bridge, shifting it off its foundation. It would be days until a temporary bridge could be installed.

Kevin was able to get town on the railroad tracks, picked up my medication, and soon I was up and active again.

Chapter 6
Friday, March 21, 1997

> Volunteering is the ultimate exercise in democracy.
> You vote in elections once a year,
> but when you volunteer,
> you vote every day about
> the kind of community you want to live in.
> —Marjorie Moore

↖↑↗

We're making a quilt together.

Actually, I am standing by as an adviser. Michael has a design in mind, knows how to measure, cut and sew. We are cutting up denim from old jeans. He has light blue, dark blue, grey and black cut into squares and triangles for the geometric pattern he drew on graph paper.

I'm so happy to be working together on this project. I have never had a teenage son! I love teamwork. It's a new adventure.

But, I'm sad, too. The quilt is for his dorm room. Michael is going away this fall.

Elise phoned home last September as soon as she was settled in at the Bonnie Hills Church School. "Please let Michael come next year. Don't make him wait. There are so many good things about this place!"

Academics, sports, clubs, music, theatre, trips, dorm life, dating, mentors. You name it. Excellent experiences are available there that Kevin and I could never provide here.

Tuition, room and board, travel expenses, clothing, sports equipment, medical insurance, school supplies. How could we possibly afford all of this without help from others? Grants make all the difference. Wealthy alumni, as well as everyday people, show their appreciation with monetary donations which provide for the next generation of students to come for this multi-faceted experience.

I was raised in this same environment in one of the smaller Church Communities in Ontario. I love the ethic of volunteering and striving for excellence while helping others that the Seer-Church emphasizes. This is part of the thread of religious instruction woven into every subject and recreational experience.

"Heaven is a Kingdom of Uses," the Seer wrote in his 40 volumes. "They who are in the love of doing uses to the community and to society, enjoy happiness above all others in heaven." The Seer describes the many times his spiritual eyes were opened. For over 26 years he was given experiences of life in Heaven. The impact of this view of Life After Death shapes the intention of every teacher, coach, dormitory staff, and clergyman and is a message the students at Bonnie Hills hear again and again.

Certainly, the idea of participating in society as an active, positive, volunteer on projects which benefit the community is

Friday, March 21, 1997

a big part of what Kevin and I value. I am glad to send our children to this place, however much it hurts my heart to see them go so far from home. Yet, since this is the core of what we strive for in our home, I am sure it will be a worthwhile building block not only for their academic education but, more importantly, for the moral and spiritual development of their character.

So, we sew.

Michael has been attending the Clearwater high school. Now he's home for Spring Break. The sunshine is slowly increasing and carving away the snowbanks. We have time for one more cozy indoor project before the flurry of springtime work on our homestead begins.

The quilt will be bulky. No batting is needed. When the denim pieces are all together, I'll show Michael how to use a regular bed sheet and tie red yarn to connect the quilt front to the sheet backing.

Who else in the boy's dormitory will have a quilt that they made themselves?

My heart feels like a roller coaster. With each successful stage of the project, I know Michael is closer to the day he will make an exit. Am I really going to let my fifteen-year-old son travel across the continent and live away from home? I weigh the pros and cons. What can we offer him here? What will he gain if he goes? When Kevin and I planned this rugged lifestyle, we did not intend to limit our children's opportunities. We wanted them to achieve and explore and know how to function in both the wilderness and the city.

Every Mother will someday release her son. Tears are expected. What a huge effort it is to raise a son! What a short time we are together! What adventures lie ahead?

In what ways will my life continue after he's gone?

March Chapter 6

↖↑↗

As often happens, either while I do hand sewing, or before I fall asleep, or sometimes in the middle of the night, or when I first wake up in the morning, my mind travels through the hallways of memory.

How did I first begin to volunteer?

I suppose it all started simply by being a big sister, way back before I can even remember clearly. As a toddler I was running and fetching for my Mother while she looked after my twin baby brothers. Later, I followed her example and learned nursery rhymes to entertain my younger sisters. Certainly I was eager to be my Mother's assistant over and over again. I remember helping in the kitchen, watching after the little ones in the backyard, or the back seat, or the church pew, getting to the school bus on time, preparing for an outing or holiday, doing chores on Saturday room cleaning day. If I saw a need that I knew how to help with, I took action.

Opportunities to volunteer came often when we lived in the Arbour Vale Church Community in Ontario. I lit the seven candles on the chancel before Sunday service. I set the table for 50 people attending the Friday supper. I ironed costumes for the annual stage play. I helped decorate the church with flowers for Easter, with harvest fruits and vegetables for Thanksgiving, with towering trees, red ribbons and white candles for Christmas. I was a Sunday School teacher. I played the clarinet to accompany the organist for special services. I directed the Christmas Tableaux. I did my part. I thrived on the teamwork and sense of belonging.

When Kevin entered the scene, we were both sixteen years old. Right away he joined the activities I was involved with. If I needed a ladder, electrical wiring, strong muscles to lift, or help cleaning up when the event was over, there was Kevin

Friday, March 21, 1997

seeing what needed to be done and offering his skillful participation. If I had an idea but didn't know how to solve the problems to bring the dream to become a reality, there was Kevin, listening, suggesting, designing, and making things happen.

"Yes," my eyes and smile expressed gratitude as I met his gaze. "Yes, that's what I imagined! Thank-you!"

"Might be a handy guy to have around," I thought as I realized I would someday leave home and need a skillful, helpful, community-minded husband.

When the Grand River flooded, Kevin and I spent a day in a nearby town slogging through a smelly, muddy basement apartment, lifting soggy furniture, scraping sediment off the floor, removing a dead fish from inside the TV. Working hard together seemed to me to be an accurate demonstration of his determination. Better than dinner and a movie and the stylized behaviour of going on a date, I could see his character. We made a solid team.

↖↑↗

At age 20, as we approached our wedding date, people asked me, "What are your plans?" There was a very strong expectation for young couples to remain in the Seer-Church Community, raise a family, participate in the annual celebrations, grow the Church. But, we had our reasons for leaving, as well as goals we wanted to strive for. Southern Ontario had rolling hills covered with forest or cleared for cornfields. I wanted to live in the mountains.

"I want to get married, go out west, build a log cabin, raise a bunch of kids, teach them about the Lord, volunteer in my community and then write a book about it." That was my answer. That was my dream. We chose to live in Avola deliberately because we could offer our skills to the children, elderly, neighbours and visitors to our community.

Kevin agreed to be the major wage earner and encouraged me to seek volunteer opportunities and take action where ever I could be of service. Kevin's reliable income meant that my needs were provided for and I was free to use my creativity in whatever way I could find. I felt like I had a wealthy benefactor!

↖↑↗

From the beginning, in addition to the homesteading lifestyle and raising our four children, my volunteer work became, and continues to be, the central purpose around which my interests revolve. I began with volunteering at the Avola elementary school, and later offered my skills to five other schools. The 'Moms and Tots' play group, Sunday School and experiences with the Brownies strengthened my leadership skills. With the other women, I also focused on the Community Hall events and Christmas Concert. Later, the local government provided a library and I created summer reading programs to keep the children active and learning.

Volunteering has always been a huge part of life for everyone who lives in Avola. "Do you need anything in town?" neighbours ask, especially in wintertime when snow, ice and poor visibility can make the roads too risky to make the trip. There are volunteer committees to look after the Hall, recreation, water system, cemetery and parks. A women's group organized an 'Avola Cookbook.' The men arrive quickly when fire threatens a neighbour's home. The school children know that the effort they make to raise money for charities connects them to other volunteers supporting an important cause.

Friday, March 21, 1997

One year a list was complied naming every person who had given volunteer time to the town. Yes, every single resident had made some contribution.

↖↑↗

When new people move into town, their interests bring new possibilities. The couple who moved in across the road from the Avola log Schoolhouse had the sound equipment, records and volunteered to teach and call square dancing! There were six young people and two adults ready to learn.

Honour your partner, honour your corner.
All join hands and circle left.
Swing your partner.
Do-si-do your corner.
Alemand left, Grand Chain.

The rhythm, smiles, mistakes and challenges, refreshments and "See you next week," combined to weave a strong bond. If someone was absent, that did not prevent the formation of the square. One person had a broom for a partner. Easy enough.

One memorable evening, two people were away. How could we make a square of eight if there were only six dancers? The broom and the mop were both enlisted, paper smiles and eyes were added to depict a cheerful personality. Halfway through the Grand Chain, left hand, right hand, left hand... stop! Whatever could be the problem? This was a figure we could all do smoothly? Turning to see where the problem might be, we all burst out laughing. Mr. Broom and Lady Mop were face-to-face, but, since they had no arms, no one could proceed!

↖↑↗

Meanwhile, being a Mother is 100% a volunteer job! Lots of work. Endless hours. No pay. Staying home full-time was my choice and part of what Kevin and I agreed on long before we were married. I wanted to pour everything I had into our children. Heart. Spirit. Mind. Body. Each needs to be nourished, stimulated to improve, find meaningful tasks to develop and grow, and choose ways to be of service to others.

↖↑↗

While we homeschooled, we also took the school bus once a week to go to Blue River. The children participated in class. I continued to volunteer, reading aloud, listening to young readers, bringing science or art projects, leading singing, helping with a skit, or fair, or sports day.

Some years our children attended school full-time. I still took the school bus one day per week to volunteer. The time I gave was amply rewarded with smiles, participation in interesting projects and that golden sense of belonging in the community.

For a few short, sweet years, we participated in a local homeschooling support group in Clearwater. I rode with all four of our children on the school bus every Friday. We arranged to tour the police station, hospital, post office and bakery. We enjoyed rides on a dogsled, learned about an old mine and planned to meet at the lake. We met every Friday at the Star Lake School building. We had the use of computers and a photocopier. The students developed a little newspaper. We had a semi-retired teacher to guide activities. She organized 'Readers Theatre' and science projects. I brought art and music. Other parents shared their expertise.

Friday, March 21, 1997

Together we planned a year end Medieval Festival. One of the Dads was the Town Crier, announcing events and serving as the Master of Ceremonies. The King and Queen presided over the festivities (Kevin wearing a white tunic and red sash, and I wearing a white long dress). It was a sunny May morning and the green lawn of the school yard was a perfect setting.

First, a quintet of young children played an 'air band' performing with recorders, a small harp and pretend lute while a cassette tape recording entertained with a lively tune. Next, a line dance and a circle dance brought people in every age group into the fun. One of the Dads had been teaching sword play to the boys with safe homemade shields and protective hockey equipment. The Tournament was made more interesting because each Lady present could encourage the Lad of her choice by giving him a flower or kerchief. The youngest children were the Court Jesters and had practised a tumbling routine.

Every person had dressed in medieval garb: long gowns, leggings wrapped, bodices laced, men in capes. We had also agreed to address each other as "M' Lord" and "M' Lady."

At noontime, the lawn became a market place. Each family brought one food item. In order to enjoy a full meal, each person had to barter with the others. "I'll trade you my bread for some of your cheese?"

A May Pole provided fun in the afternoon, again with a cassette tape bringing music to set the pace.

At the end of the day, my smile muscles were sore!

The following year my major contribution to the Friday homeschooling gathering was choreographing 'The Seven Days of Creation Dance.' The gym was set up for theatre-in-the-round. I felt like I had reached the pinnacle of my volunteer leadership.

⇖↑⇗

News travels by word of mouth up and down the valley. I heard that a teacher in Clearwater at the Raft River Elementary School was preparing a production of *Joseph and the Amazing Technicolor Dreamcoat*. I made a phone call. "I would like to volunteer in any way at all. I will fold programs. I will stack chairs. I will sweep the floor. But, I would love to do the choreography. I have known this music since I was twelve years old. I would love to come to the school and see what might be possible with the Grade 6 and 7 students?"

That phone call changed my life. No longer was I volunteering in tiny Avola with no other adult to witness the children's delight at learning. I stepped out into a wider world. Over the next three years, I volunteered with several hundred children, choreographed six plays, gained a reputation, and best of all, gained confidence.

"How did you do that?" the teachers quietly asked me. They wanted to know what educational method or model I was following. From this, I began to build the 'Seven Predictable Patterns®'[13] seminars.

⇖↑⇗

By now, Elise and Michael were getting older and their opportunities were expanding. I didn't volunteer at the high school, but I did go on field trips with the high school band as a chaperone. The music teacher insisted I join the band! I rented a clarinet and was surprised to realize that my fingers could remember what to do! I saw the Parliament Buildings in Victoria, BC, and toured the Butchart Gardens. The students stayed at the University of Victoria and the Simon Fraser

Friday, March 21, 1997

University dormitories. The school band also went to several small schools across Highway 24 and north to Prince George.

༺↑༻

When I eventually overcame my reluctance and earned my driver's license, I was strongly motivated by the realization that I would be able to volunteer in more activities more frequently and travel farther away.

After our homeschooling studies, I drove to Clearwater so Nicholas and Toby could join Cub Scouts. I chaperoned for their big trip. We slept in Vancouver's Science World and toured the aquarium.

༺↑༻

Through the grapevine I heard the teacher of the primary grades was taking her class to Kamloops to hear *Peter and the Wolf*. "May I visit your classroom and prepare the children to recognize the story, instruments and theme music?" With stick puppets and singing each part, I re-told the classic Russian tale. The children turned to me in the darkened theatre. "It's the duck!" and "I hear the cat!"

༺↑༻

Some of my family and friends questioned my priorities. "How can you afford to live on one wage?" and "Why do you give away so much time?"

Meals, transportation, lodging and other expenses are covered for chaperones on field trips. Tickets to concerts, training for First Aide and teacher's Professional Development Days have all been paid for because I volunteer. Socializing with professionals and other volunteers strengthens my dedication, provides education, and also benefits my own professional skills.

A conference in Vancouver and a fun weekend in Valemount for Girl Guide leaders refreshed and inspired me. 'Peace' was the theme for a Girl Guide camp and I was invited to provide music, dance and a quilting project. Although separated by distance, I was able to participate in monthly Guide Leaders' meetings by using the speaker phone.

I excelled at literary, musical and creative projects.

↖↑↗

Meanwhile, Kevin's volunteer work involved life-and-death decisions. His ongoing training and activities provided Search and Rescue, Highway Rescue, First Aid and Amateur Radio communication to the region we live in. Because it takes nearly an hour for the ambulance and police to arrive at a highway accident, because Kevin is on the road during all weathers, because he is familiar with the back roads, mountain topography and river crossings, his contribution has had a significant impact on the outcome of many emergency events.

↖↑↗

What Happened Next?

At the end of the following school year, in 1998, I accepted an invitation to speak at the Bonnie Hills Church School ceremony for Elise's graduating class. Besides the thrill of returning to my own Alma Mater, touring the facilities and seeing the denim quilt Michael made in his dormitory room, the once-in-a-lifetime experience of witnessing our firstborn graduate, the privilege of speaking to the assembled dignitaries, teachers,

Friday, March 21, 1997

students and parents, Kevin and I were also given all-expenses paid air fare.

Yes, there are unexpected and welcome benefits to being a volunteer.

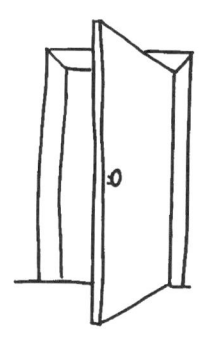

Chapter 7
Tuesday, February 28, 2006

> Be a first-rate version
> of yourself,
> instead of a second-rate version
> of somebody else.
> —Judy Garland

↘↓↙

I have been travelling.

A lot.

In our extended family, if one relative needs an extra adult, the request is passed around until someone is found who can drop their own responsibilities to come and help out. A cousin goes to England to look after small children for six weeks while their mother is in cancer treatments. An uncle goes to live with a family when the third child is born. Grampa Hinkle came to our house to take us on outings before I earned my driver's license. Dearma has attended her daughters, Julie, Carol and l during childbirth, staying on to help with domestic duties for up to six weeks. A daughter welcomes her mother into her home while the older woman recovers from a hysterectomy. Three sisters rotate 24-hour duties as they attend Oma as she slowly fades and leaves this life. Weddings bring cousins together. Family reunions are planned. Christmas greetings exchanged. We live in three countries and fifteen states, but we somehow feel connected.

Now that my own children are away at school or all grown up, I can be the 'extra adult' when needed. I have been a Nanny for each of my siblings' families. James and Lily, near London, were focused on writing a book. I took their children to the park to feed the swans. Andrew and Lisa, near New York City, had children with different school holidays at spring break. I got the be the Auntie who took them to museums, libraries and playgrounds. Julie and Ted, near Denver, took a holiday to Spain. I walked their three children to the school bus. Carole and Jim, near Philadelphia, took a professional development seminar in Hawaii. I made sure their three children had a pleasant time while they were away. A cousin recently miscarried. I offered to do all the cleaning and lifting so she could rest. A widowed aunt, near Raleigh, had to empty her home. I listened to her describe the gardens, wood working and home improvements her husband had made for her. A classmate, near Los Angeles, discovered her sixth child was born with a medical condition. I loaded laundry, washed dishes, read aloud and kept the meals coming while she went to doctor's appointments and waited anxiously for test results. A cousin, near Seattle, attended a wedding in Texas. I made soup with her two sons. A friend hired me to go to Atlanta to work for her mother. The narrow pathways through her stacks of boxes, stuffed closets, heaps of clothing and shelves piled with clutter were reduced to order within ten days.

Tuesday, February 28, 2006

The usual arrangement is that the host family pays for the helper's airfare, provides room and board, and offers a small allowance. It is an arrangement I quite enjoy.

↘↓↙

I am in Brooklyn now. I have agreed to be the Auntie for a whole year for this family while their Dad has a rotation of business trips overseas every few weeks. Their Mom has a fast-paced career in Manhattan. They have a marvellous Nanny for after school. I have come to help during the early morning rush to get everyone out the door on time, as well as relieve the pressure to get supper and bedtime managed efficiently. The middle of the day is all mine.

I can walk along Flatbush Avenue and wander into the shops. I can take the subway to Central Park. I can see the Christmas windows along 5th Avenue. I can ride the elevator up Rockefeller Centre. I can say, "I've been there!" when I watch movies set in New York City. I can take the ferry to the Statue of Liberty. I pause to hear buskers play trumpets in Battery Park. I am surprised to hear those Caribbean metal drums in the subway stations. I can stroll through Tiffany's and imagine wearing the sparkling jewels, ropes of pearls, ornate medallions, heavy pendants, delicate earrings and golden bracelets. I can feast my eyes on paintings and sculptures in the Metropolitan Museum of Art. I can see a matinée on Broadway. I can return to the Museum of Natural History, where I went as a child, and see the elephants, lions, birds and baboons in still-life scenes. After seeing the animal displays, I can go into the dark room where brightly lit gems are arranged. Star sapphires and opals, rubies and garnets, emeralds and amethyst, turquoise and tiger's eye, both raw and cut, from the lightest pastel tints to the deepest rich shades. I can mount the Empire State Building and recall holding Oma's white gloved hand when I was a child.

I have a library card! I can bring home the wealth of literature, knowledge, biographies, poetry and of course, brightly illustrated tales for the children. I can explore pathways in parks, join fitness classes, dance, soak up music. I can go swimming in a pool located on the 7th floor of the Synagogue, just above the preschool! I can eat foods from Africa, Sweden, Italy, Japan, India, Mexico. I can see people and places in real life that I have previously only seen on TV.

I can participate at the Food Co-op; answering the phone (there is a thick notebook of info so I can accurately answer questions), stocking the shelves (who knew there is such a thing as sheep milk yogourt), cutting and wrapping the cheese (so many interesting smells), arranging the vegetables and fruits (colours, shapes, textures and flavours unfamiliar to me).

I can go with the little boys to extra lessons and meet the music teacher, violin instructor, tennis coach, Mandarin tutor. I can watch their soccer practice, hear their school concert, go to their church, visit where the parents work. I can go with our Nanny and meet up with other Nannies, each with a preschooler holding onto the stroller with a baby buckled in. I can hear them tell of the speech therapist, music therapist, occupational therapist or physiotherapist where they take the children to blow bubbles, wear a weighted vest, pick up tiny buttons, repeat vowel and consonant sounds, clap or stomp or drum in rhythm.

New York is, of course, somewhat overwhelming. A zillion people. Each with a zillion hopes and dreams and careers and lifestyles. I see homeless people asleep in doorways and on stairs. I see fur coats and diamonds on ladies stepping out of black limousines, their uniformed drivers holding the door with tinted windows. I see faces of every age and shade of

Tuesday, February 28, 2006

pink and brown, golden and black. I see hair in dread-locks and braids, Hebrew curls and bushy beards, dyed and spiked, shaved and wrapped in turbans. Everyone in the world is here. Once my taxi driver was from Egypt. Another was from Brazil.

I am here, too, in New York City, surrounded by millions of people. I come from Avola, inhabited by less that 50 people. But, (and this is a secret) I am not sure if I am going back.

↘↓↙

My children have all left home. There are no children left in all of Avola. My husband is away from home ten hours each day. I have no possible way to earn money. I have to travel to another town to find ways to volunteer. I can't ride the school bus anymore. If I am not earning a wage, how can I possibly I pay for a car? repairs? insurance? gas? I dread the long winters. I am tired of the isolation. I hunger for people and activities, learning and participation. I want to join clubs, go to church, engage in interesting conversation. Is it too much to ask to have activities I enjoy on my calendar?

I still have my United States citizenship. I really could find a position as a live-in-Nanny. I really could find a way to support myself.

Returning to Avola? My husband is there. My garden is there. The lifestyle I thought I wanted is there. But. The whole thing feels like an endurance test.

↘↓↙

During my travels, I have been picking up brochures from places and programs where I think I could find employment. With a little bit of training or a few years of education, could I take on an entirely different life in a place filled with opportunities?

What if I had married a different man? What if I decide now to choose a different Path?

Surely all of my volunteer training and experience has added up to some kind of employable skills?

Brooklyn seems bursting with opportunities for me. 'Brooklyn Family' is a free newspaper offering science and sports, music and entertainment, parent training and a summer camp. 'Brooklyn Parent' is another free magazine and web page with ads and a calendar of events including Infant CPR, a family dance, international cultural clubs with annual celebrations. 'Park Slope Parent' specifically highlights information and local opportunities for family centred outings. 'Linewaiters Gazette' is the food co-op newspaper announcing creative classes, writers workshops, dance groups, and food and farmer info. Recycling suggestions and environmental issues are also topics of interest.

The library has programs for tots. I could be reading aloud for pay. The Brooklyn Children's Museum has programs and birthday parties scheduled. I could transform my homeschooling skills into creative learning for pay. The art gallery has registration for 'Grandparents Day' coming up. I could combine my love of both age groups into projects for pay. Literacy groups, public speaking groups, folk dance groups, homeschooling groups are all looking for leaders who get paid. Parent Education is a big topic, supporting families, encouraging holiday traditions, singing and touching and reading together, cooking together, roll-and-tumble play, face-to-face play, strengthening and passing on faith traditions. These are the things I care about. These people are getting paid. Private schools need teacher's aides. Public schools need after school programs. Creative and artistic and musical individuals are self-employed as therapists, consultants, coaches, entertainers, tutors.

Tuesday, February 28, 2006

This could be ME!

If this city is too hectic and fast paced for me, I could go live in Colorado, where I grew up. There are fourteen branches of the Colorado Springs libraries with storytelling, Mom-and-Tot story-time, play-time, art contest, movie Monday, Seniors Luncheon, holiday crafts, and meetings for parent support groups.

This could be ME!

In the Church communities in Ontario, Pennsylvania and other places, there are small schools with meeting rooms and libraries and after school programs, each with the potential for more creative educational activities, tutors, child care and parent support employees.

This could be ME!

In Seattle, I picked up numerous brochures.

It seems to me that where ever I travel, every city is expanding programs for early child development.

This could be ME!

Colleges and adult training centres offer courses I could take and get qualifications. Small Business start-up coaching is available in my own province in Canada.

This could be ME!

It is all impossible if I live in Avola. It is all possible if I leave home.

Is this sense of longing and yearning an indication to pursue these ideas? Or is it a temptation to be resisted? I try to see down either path. It is not possible to see the future clearly, but I can make a guess.

Divorce is something I do not want to consider. It is not Kevin I want to leave. My relationship with him is not the problem. His kind, honest, loyal character qualities are reliable. But, he is not going to budge. He also will not stop me if I want to invent some kind of long-distance marriage. My own hesitation is the only thing stopping me.

↘↓↙

I am spending a lot of time and creativity imagining different scenarios.

But, this is now. Today is today. And, I have a plan for myself while the family does not need me.

February has been icy with hazardous sidewalks preventing a brisk stride. But, March is coming, and I can venture out for a longer walk. The trees and plants are beginning to awaken. Under the ground, inside the trunks and bulbs, I know there is hidden potential. Limitations are becoming possibilities. No more waiting for this part of the cycle to fade.

I am headed to the Brooklyn Botanical Gardens. I have been there before. And yet, really, every time is a first time. Free admission every Tuesday draws me to enter repeatedly.

Walking along permanent prescribed paths during these last days of winter, searching for the first signs of spring in this place of abundance and variety and awareness, I breathe in deeply the chilly, damp air. The icy patches on the walkways are receding. The shrinking piles of melting snow releases the faint scent of mud, grass, moss and the buds of the many trees. In the monochromatic landscape, it is possible to notice the twigs blushing red, the buds swelling green, the life in the sap beginning to be drawn upwards by the returning golden sunshine. My senses open wide. Not only my eyes and ears, but also my internal senses notice messages and meanings.

Leaving behind the press of the stone apartment buildings, the towering glass office buildings, the massive Brooklyn Library near the entrance of Prospect Park, the white museum columns, I pass through the Eastern Parkway Gate. "Free

Tuesday, February 28, 2006

admission Tuesday?" I pause to make eye contact with the guard in his glass enclosure. He smiles and nods. I take a map from the display, although I know my way, there is always something new to learn.

Last summer, thick greenery clothed the vine-entwined pergolas along the wide walkway. The romantic canopy of draped wisteria gave the impression of a royal welcome. Now, the writhing trunks are bare. Will the misty veil of purple hues return? February is a time of waiting, believing, hoping after so many chilly nights and dreary days of cloudy no-sky.

The fountain is a cupcake of white snow. I smile to remember playing here with the children last year. I anticipate bringing them again this year. When the snow melts, I will toss a penny in and make a wish as is the universal custom evidenced by the sparkling coins in the shallow stone basin.

I pause at the overlook. I know exactly where I am. I have arrived.

↘↓↙

I am such a long way from home. Gladly, I travelled by bus through the mountains overnight for eight hours to get to Vancouver, then by Sky Train to the airport. After the first flight, I transferred to another airline. At the La Guardia airport, I boarded a city bus to Penn Station and at last, found the platform to board the subway, stepped off at the familiar station, to finally walk one block, climb eleven stairs, and knock on the door. Hurrah for extended family!

How wealthy I am to have a husband who so willingly looks after himself while I am away from home. How wealthy I am to have a family who so willingly exchanged the price of my ticket for the Nanny work I will do for them this year. What a contrast between this densely populated city and my tiny mountain village. How splendid to be welcomed by the children. It is a huge relief to the family to have my steady and reliable presence.

↘↓↙

Now that I am oriented, here, I can fully focus on the details in this world-class Botanical Garden.

Straight ahead is a stairway leading down into the amazingly diverse Cranford Rose Garden. When I first arrived last September, I stopped again and again to savour the sweetness, to find a favourite fragrance, to admire the shades of yellow, pink, peach, white, deep red. Until then, I had no idea that even the size of roses is variable. Tiny ruffled miniatures so softly pink, medium sized buds boldly yellow-orange, wide spread white petals with each tip a surprisingly bright magenta. There are heritage and brand new varieties. Carefully pruned, supported by lattices, accurately labelled, the information signs say that a thousand types of roses have been collected here to be enjoyed by visitors from all over the world.

But, today the tangle of thorns has no signs of life. I turn left to walk the slope downward towards one of my favourite parts of the garden. Although there are plants here from all over the world and most of them I am unfamiliar with, here, in the Herb Garden I recognize some of the foliage, many of the names of the plants and their uses. I even have some of them in my garden at home.

Low, clipped shrubbery outlines an interlocking geometric pattern like a triple Celtic knot. Narrow pathways allow the visitor to read the signs marking the culinary, medicinal, poisonous, fragrant and ornamental plants. Some plants are used for smoking, drinking and flavouring. Although there are only brown and grey spikes and curled, dry leaves poking up through the snow, I still like to read the names.

In my kitchen I have: horseradish, parsley, celery, leek, cardamon, caraway, oregano, ginger, asparagus, thyme, licorice.

In my garden I have: rhubarb, onion, mint, garlic, chives, kohlrabi, kale, strawberry, plantain, thistle, raspberry, lemon balm.

In my medicine chest I have: St. John's Wort, witch hazel, horehound, valerian, senna, wormwood.

I have nowhere near the total here of 300 plants, still, I feel connected to this knowledge of plant life, cultivation, harvest and uses.

To the right, a few steps further along, is the entrance to the Japanese pond and hill garden. The covered benches offer a resting place. I think I will come back on a warmer day with coloured pencils and a tablet to sketch. Today I notice that bamboo and evergreens, even in winter, share their textures and year-round beauty. The man-made features include the shrine, stone statues, a lantern-like structure and bridge. They contrast and compliment the rock, waterfall, grasses and ground cover. The traditional orange torii in the middle of the pond is a symbolic gateway marking the transition from the mundane to the sacred. I can see why. I think I have stepped from Earth to Heaven.

In a few weeks, cherry blossoms will swell and open and other flowers will paint the scene throughout the warmer months. Under the ice, the large, orange and white speckled koi fish wait for the tourists to scatter crumbs. Somehow, somewhere, the turtles, too, are waiting to enjoy the sun on logs and rocks along the shore line.

In what ways am I dormant? Waiting? What resources within me are hibernating? What stimulation might I need to blossom and overflow with colour and creativity?

February Chapter 7

Reluctantly, I exit the shelter, yet, I am eager to see if there are signs of life in the Shakespeare Garden. Tall evergreens enclose this cozy space, block any distraction from view and create privacy. The brick path is clear of snow. Various supports of basket-like wicker and cane stakes forecast how the withered plants will soon revive and reach to the sun, spreading green. Simple labels declare the old English name, the botanical Latin name and the reference to Shakespeare's writing where the plant was mentioned.

A chart is near the entrance, posting the symbolic meanings of the flowers. It makes me curious about this language of lovers, and dangerous curses, and secret messages which might be delivered in a bouquet. What do my favourite flowers mean? Our wedding daisies mean 'innocence and hope'! My Oma had a frame with pressed, white Edelweiss meaning 'courage and devotion.' I do love a forest floor of ferns, a symbol of 'sincerity.' Lilac, to me means 'spring is here' and is listed as 'joy of youth.' Common white clover means 'think of me.'

Tiny green spears have pierced the snow. Hyacinth? Tulip? Snow-drops! They're alive! So fragile, tiny and brave! I'm surprised to find colour! The purple, closed crocus will bloom tomorrow if it is warm. Sun warms a large rock, bringing spring conditions early. Daffodils suddenly announce, "Yes! Spring is just around the corner."

But, 'Daffodil Hill' is shaded by the giant oak and is not warm enough yet. I will come next Tuesday. And the week after. And continue to make this pilgrimage regularly until I witness the carpet of gold, like a skirt made of sunshine under the enormously wide spreading oak giant. I'll have to wait until April when the daffodils will spill down the hill, so delicate in contrast to the massive tree.

The lily ponds are dormant. The trees, silent now, will soon sing. In May, the cherry blossoms waft sweetness across the lawn. The vegetable gardens, available to school children, are still. But, there are indoor gardens to explore. So, I press on.

Specimens from the whole wide world live in this glass-enclosed collection. There are actually four separate ecosystems, each with their own astonishing display. The Aquatic House is hot and humid, just right for swamp loving flowers and vines. The Tropical Pavilion houses trees, ferns and thick clusters of jungle plants crowding their greenery in the heat. The Desert Pavilion is hot and dry. Cactus surprise me with their variations. So small, so huge, so prickly, they somehow survive in the red gravel soil. The Warm Temperate Pavilion reproduces the cool climate for high altitude plants. Tiny flowers, unusual leaves, clumps and clusters, vines and mosses, low bushes and tall stems.

And after a stroll, a pause to drink in the wonder and enjoyment, there is one more place to explore. I save the Bonsai greenhouse for last. I like to linger here. I don't know why, but these individual plants fascinate me.

Each miniature tree is displayed on its own table in its own small dish. A tag states how old it is. A poster explains how the gardener has limited the tree's growth by trimming away the tiny roots, preventing the tree from gathering enough nourishment to grow to its full size. Wires shape the branches as the gardener wishes. Great care is taken. These trees are 70-150 years old!

Sometimes when I visit, the whole thing seems grotesque. Deliberately reducing resources? How cruel! Why don't the trees shrivel and starve? If they could call out would they moan, or whine, or grumble, or beg?

Sometimes when I visit, my eyes soak in the wonder and beauty and abundance of each tree. Soil, water, air, light. Separately, they are inanimate. Together they produce Life!

Each tree is a perfect miniature example of 'The Best Version of My Tree-Self.'

Today I have a sudden sensation.

I am looking at myself! These trees are a portrait, a mirror, a parallel.

At some times in my life I have had such limited resources. Not enough money, food, warmth, light, hugs, art supplies, time, energy, intellectual stimulation, community. I live in a place at such a great distance from my family. Would the limitations crush me? Would I wither and weaken? Would I turn my face downward and become bitter? Would I moan, or whine, or grumble, or beg? Or, like these trees, would the limitations actually help me trim away unnecessary luxuries? Would I be able to focus and become 'The Best Version of *My* Self'?

Each tiny tree is still its own kind of tree. It is not crippled or deformed or harmed. It is still singing its own song. The gardener cannot stop it from being what it is meant to be. Small. But complete.

All of those career ambitions and self-employment potentials I have been considering as if they were far away and out of reach? I have done each of these things in tiny little Avola: library, speech, dance, music, church, Brownies, Nanny, seminars, theatre.

I am who I am. I do what I do.

I wish I had a title, credentials, an income, an office, a diploma on the wall.

I do not have those things to prove that my achievements have value. But, they do.

My camera preserves the image of the Bonsai trees. My journal records my thoughts and realization. My heart has shifted away from the lifeless winter, desolate and barren. Springtime warms my heart. I see myself as fruitful. Oriented to my own Path, when my work here is finished, I can return to my home and husband, my own particular limitations and possibilities.

↘↓↙

What Happened Next?

"Get on the phone, Eleanor," Cheryl sent me an email in mid-May. "I'm at a meeting and they're talking about hiring a 'Super Nanny' here in Clearwater! I think it should be you!"

First I called Cheryl. Then I called the Social Worker. I was hired! They wanted me to come right away.

"Be careful what you wish for," Kevin said. He knew how much I wanted to bring parenting skills to young families.

It was perfect timing. This job put all of my parenting skills to the test.[14] It was extremely enjoyable.

I stood on a plateau and looked out over my life with a deep satisfaction and realized that the paid and volunteer work I have done has made a difference in a great many families.

Chapter 7
Tuesday, March 27, 2007

> We are a vibration
> in a note of God's concerto.
> —*Author Unknown*

↖↑↗

I was a little skeptical.

I have observed many teachers in classrooms. I have observed physical therapists, occupational therapists, speech therapists, psychologists and teacher's aids. It seems like all of them have an agenda, a clip board, a series of evaluations, a list of learning out-comes and goals, and specific ways they want to use their skills to address the child's difficulties and see some kind of on-going, measurable improvement.

But, music therapy? What is that?

I was a little defensive.

The child I care for is very precious and cheerful. I feel like protecting him from fault finding or any pressure on him to hurry up or begin to doubt his own ability. I love to stimulate his creativity, watch him enjoy the world, listen to his observations and questions and allow his play to morph from one thing to another without watching the clock.

What can music therapy hope to accomplish?

I was a little doubtful.

I have seen the flash of understanding on this little boy's face. I have seen his satisfaction of doing something well, with no anticipation of praise from any adult. I don't want him to be manipulated, expected to copy a routine, mimic the leader and produce some false reading on a chart.

Is music therapy the latest cure-all, trendy, snake oil?

I was a little protective.

I know that when I volunteer with children, their loyalty and affection is a treasure. I am extremely careful, knowing that what I say and do, my attitudes and behaviours leave a lasting impression. It is a big responsibility.

Who is this therapist? How will he interact with this child?

I was about to meet a music therapist named Jon Samson.

When I first heard the name, two weeks ago, and imagined a person with a career as Music Therapist, I pictured a kindly old man with a white beard (somewhat unkempt), wearing a brown tweed suit (frayed at the knees and elbows), a tan vest (that didn't meet around his middle-aged middle) a white shirt (was that a spot of mustard) and a green bow-tie (a little crooked). His twinkling eyes and nodding head would signal 'welcome' but his distant gaze would indicate the 'absent minded professor' mode of communicating.

I was very curious.

What does a music therapist do? Who are his clients? What difference does the hour they spend together make to the client? How can the therapist know if his work is... well... therapeutic?

Tuesday, March 27, 2007

I imagined that his place of work would be half office (creaky wooden floor, old wooden desk, stacks and layers of papers and folders) and half music studio (a piano, a cello, a few foreign drums, portraits of the great composers). His clients would be reluctant, withdrawn. He would coax and demonstrate, hum and clap, expecting them to mimic him, or smile, or participate in some small way. He would patiently, but ineffectively spend an hour and make an appointment for next week, reassuring the parents that their money was well spent, that their child was making progress, however slight.

What a contrast to the person, career description and observations I had when I stepped into Jon Samson's studio two weeks ago.

↖↑↗

One of the children I am looking after this year has weekly sessions with Jon. It is hoped that speech and coordination will improve. The kid likes music. The parents are anxious. Jon needs work. I asked to tag along.

Usually shy and quiet, the little boy steps out of his stroller, up the stairs and eagerly enters the room. Eye contact and greetings, introductions are first. Right away, there is music. Barely out of university, Jon Samson is lean, sports a tuft of new beard, and is about the same age as my children! Full of energy, dressed in jeans and a t-shirt, most comfortable sitting on the floor with his ukulele, Jon is not going to make this kid do things 'the right way.' I see that Jon is listening, respectful of the person this small lad is. Without allowing the child to be demanding, he is allowing the child to lead.

The ukulele is small. The 'Hello' song is familiar. A question is posed. "Would you like to be the conductor?" The lad nods, measures the rhythm with a real baton, and points to the piano. Jon slides onto the bench, reinforces their connection with his smiling eyes. He will follow the child's lead. Faster, slower, more intense, delicate, pizzicato, largo, all of these are indications the child gives and Jon picks up immediately. There is no gap between what the child directs and the effect they have on the music. They are making something new together that has never been made before.

The lad's focus drops, the conductor's baton goes limp, the child's eyes wander. Jon sits on the floor and sways, singing, asking, waiting for the lad's next point of interest.

The child goes to the piano, striking three notes. Jon picks up the tune and beat, adding chords and expanding on the tune. The child repeats these three notes, realizing the wealth of harmony that he started with these three tones. Meeting Jon's eyes with trust, the child realizes that he has initiated and the adult has understood.

I am astounded.

Here, the Client is not expected to copy, or be instructed by, or corrected by the Therapist. This little boy has had enough of that from the other teachers, tutors and adults in his life. Slumped and unresponsive, he is used to 'failure.' It is difficult to tell if he is learning anything because he is so withdrawn in the 'do it this way' environment. Here, I can see, he is thriving.

Now the music is coaxing the child to begin to move. He leaves the keyboard, while Jon continues the spontaneous composition, keeping the regularity of the beat and tune, but now, adding flourishes and trills. The child is clearly thrilled. Without speaking he tosses me a glance signalling, "Look what I made!" The piano brings a bold beat. Marching and clapping increases the child's fitness and stamina. The melody slows. Jon shifts to a minor mode. The child responds with swaying, bending his spine, head downcast, arms are extended with slower, heavier movements. When Jon runs his fingers up the scales, the child stretches upwards and makes little hops and turns.

Tired now, the little boy comes to me for a hug and a rest on my lap.

Jon reaches for the basket of rhythm instruments, allowing the child and I to choose. He briefly explains that he uses them in a call and response 'conversation.' This emphasizes the 'taking turns' part of speaking and listening.

Picking up on our names, Jon begins a chant, signalling each to take a turn. Now the lad is gaining much needed practice and confidence with his delayed speech. Because each of the other activities have been enjoyably spontaneous and the lad has never been shamed, or his efforts ignored, he is willing to try something more difficult. Because Jon has been strengthening the sense of belonging and bond of trust between them with eye contact and smiles, the lad believes in his own ability to accomplish this new task. Because the lad has been 'successful' and never has been stopped or corrected, the child eagerly repeats the chant.

The chant becomes a tune. Singing is a joy. This brings satisfaction. Circling back to repeat, Jon demonstrates good diction and keeping up the pace. The lad experiences the reassurance of doing things together. I see acceptance. I see guidance. I see invitation. I see encouragement. I see creative problem solving on the spot. This young therapist is truly 'Here' with his client. 'Now' is the only thing that matters, not past performance on a test, not future hope for progress. Simply creating brand new music together. He calls his work 'Co-Creative Music.' And, indeed, it is.

"Let's have a band!" The little one has had enough of the focused task, hunches down for a moment, then he perks up, nodding his head and moving to the beat. I take up some shakers, Jon is on the piano, the boy strums the ukulele and we sing out, making it up as we take turns.

After that first day with the music therapist, I begin gathering information from the little lad's other teachers, aids and therapists. I am able to more accurately put educational golden moments into our time together.

↖↑↗

When it was time for the next session, I felt as though I was carrying a sacred flame. Without tampering with the tune, or snuffing out the enthusiasm, or overwhelming the lad, I brought a composition from home.

"Can you play, *When the saints go marching in*? This fellow made up a song!" And Jon picks up the lively tune on the keyboard.

> *O Peter Pan, and Captain Hook!*
> (The little fellow made up this part at home, delivering it in rhythm while beating his foot on the floor)
> *O Peter Pan and Captain Hook!*
> (I repeated it, making eye contact, nodding to the beat and showing a welcoming smile on my face)
> *O how I'd love to read a book about*
> (I added this line and rhyme
> ... tossing the invitation back to him)
> *Peter Pan and Captain Hook!*
> (together we finished)

I've never seen this little boy so full of pep, energetically dancing, huge grin, eye contact flashing with the realization that he has done something grand and good.

Tuesday, March 27, 2007

I watched Jon closely. Was he showing off? Entertaining? Looking for attention? Faking his enthusiasm? His interest in this small person sure seemed authentic to me.

↖↑↗

At the end of the second session, last week, I invited Jon Samson to meet me today at the Brooklyn Botanical Gardens.
 I'm a little nervous.
 While I wait, I remind myself why I wanted to have a conversation with him. I noticed that when he was playing the piano in the studio, the guitar strings across the room were resonating. One vibration 'over there' was picked up by an instrument 'over here.' Although at a distance, the tone was the same.
 That is how I felt while Jon was leading the music therapy session. I could see that his methods and mine were so similar. I could feel a recognition of the work that I do with children, although I live all the way across the continent. First, the string was silent and separate. When the vibration travelled cross the room, the string responded, becoming the voice it was intended to be, a lovely note. From silent and withdrawn, confused and unappreciated, while observing Jon's method, I responded, becoming more clearly what I was intended to be; a voice in the wilderness with a strong message of hope to deliver to the children I volunteer with.
 I invited Jon to meet with me because I want to hear more of his philosophy and experiences. And I want to share mine.
 His long-legged stride is recognizable from a distance. The refreshment booth is not open this early in the season, but the sunshine is inviting. I brought a thermos of tea, cups and muffins to share at the patio tables.
 "Tell me all about your work. What was your education and training? How did you know you wanted to do this? Who

do you work with? Children? Adults? How do you find new clients? What other options, dreams, goals do you have? What are you thinking while you interact with these children?" I want to learn as much as possible as quickly as possible.

And I sketch my own brief biography. "I have had almost no training. I quit university twice. I have been considering going back to school and claiming a real career. I live way out in the mountains of Canada. I volunteer with children in various settings. I rarely benefit from working with and learning from other adults. I have been feeling discouraged. Sometimes the isolation is crushing. I feel like 'one hand clapping.' But, in your studio, I feel like I can see the value of my own work while I watch you work."

His laughter echoes. He leans back and soaks in the sky. He leans forward and intently looks straight into my eyes.

"What is it that you see?" He doesn't answer. He asks.

"Well, first of all, you aren't giving music 'lessons' are you? I teach, too, but not in the 'top-down' way where the teacher speaks and the child listens. The usual method is that the teacher knows and the child is empty." I try to summarize my own philosophy. "I have a plan, but I am willing to move away from my plan if I notice they have lost interest, and move towards what the children find interesting. I'm not governed by curriculum or the clock. I don't have tests or report cards. I can tell that the children are learning because they have bright eyes, eager participation and come back again the next time. "

"Exactly!" he exclaims, nodding, "We listen to each other. We know the child is bringing their own rich ideas and are full of creativity. All we do is remain available, listening, observing, our senses open to input. Our leadership comes from clues the child signals, not from our authority or superiority. We are literally co-creating. Their input is as valid as mine."

Tuesday, March 27, 2007

He continues, "I already know that children have music they carry inside. I expect to meet them there and do it their way, using my skills and talents and training and experience as a resource the children can draw on while I support what they are building as their skill and understanding develops. The only expectation is the sense of wonder and surprise that something beautiful is happening."

Jon is so new in his career. He is eager to share what he believes. "In a standard music lesson, the teacher already knows what the content, sequence and requirements will be. The student does as instructed. Or fails. In the 'Co-Creative' music experience, I already know the participant will have ideas. I listen to the rhythms, melody and tempo that the child spontaneously provides. Then I provide solid structure and enriched accompaniment while the co-creative child explores."

To be sure I understand, I feedback what I have heard. "In traditional school settings, the child's ideas are an interruption of the lesson. But I noticed with you in the co-creative method you have developed, child's ideas *are* the lesson."

"I have stayed to observe other therapists," I continue, "Speech, small motor, gross motor, tutors. It seems like the other therapies and therapists see what is 'wrong' with the child and they 'know' how to 'fix' it."

"Yes, Co-Creative therapy isn't about right and wrong, or more and less," Jon agrees. "I meet the child where they are, gladly accept this place, and together, we explore what is possible."

Jon waits. He has allowed me to ask questions. My observations are valid. My mind is open. I am gaining confidence. I sense a strong trust and respect between us. Both of us are aware of the fragile moment. Something new happening.

"Tell me about your work," he quietly coaxes.

And suddenly, bright light surrounds everything I have ever done. Babysitting and bedtime. Reading aloud and jumping rope. Play-dough and finger paint. Preschool, Sunday School, Brownies, setting up spelling bees and reading challenges at the library. Homeschooling and travel. Being a Mom. Bringing my children into academic as well as practical skills in our home and garden. Volunteering in the community to provide events and celebrations. Being a Nanny.

I tell him about the 'Seven Predictable Patterns®' seminars I have developed and the many cities I have travelled to. I tell him about the newspaper and magazine articles I have written and the conferences I have spoken at. I tell him about the homeschooling curriculum I developed and my dream of writing books. I don't feel like I am bragging. I feel like I am sharing with a colleague the exciting discoveries, achievements and creative developments of my own skill, talents and purpose.

"Come. I want to show you something," I gather the picnic things, aware of his limited time, and push open the heavy door to the greenhouse where the tables each hold one Bonsai tree.

"See these tiny trees? This is me looking in the mirror. I live in a very limited environment. But, I am still me. I can do what I do. I can be who I am."

Eye contact is a meeting of minds, like music, like honey, like a sunrise, like a welcoming hug.

He has an appointment.

I walk slowly back to the place I am staying. There is time to be still and ponder the afternoon.

༄༅༆

Does one person matter? Do I matter? Do my ideas matter? The Co-Creative answer is a resounding, 'Yes!'

Tuesday, March 27, 2007

Is my 'work' only significant if I have a university degree? If I am getting paid? The Co-Creative answer is an emphatic, 'No!'

Before the Co-Creative Music experience, I felt I was never 'good enough,' not only at music but really in any of my skills. The Co-Creative theme releases me of this heavy way to think and see myself. My contribution is valid. I am not weighted down and closed off. I don't feel burdened with the sense of shame or self-doubt, continuously asking for recognition or approval from the teacher. I have found the satisfaction to create, play, explore, just be, connect, hear what is happening. Music flows. Music flows through me. It is not an effort, a struggle, or a way to get approval or disapproval. It is music. It is possible. I can make music.

↖↑↗

I reach for the sketch tablet Journal I am drawing in every day.

A red 'heart' is central on the page. A bold golden sunshine beams down, filling the heart. This golden light is the Lord giving me abundant gifts in my heart, and stimulating my creativity. Bursting out of my heart, rays lead to multiple ways I have included music in my life. I draw a cluster of faces in a choir. I draw myself playing folk music on my guitar. Dancers leap. Children skip. Partners enjoy hand-clapping rhymes. Families sing around a bon-fire. Brownies learn rounds, and practice music for seasonal celebrations. A landscape reminds me of the many songs about the beauty of Nature. Sacred symbols remind me of hymns, Psalms, prayers and carols. I draw tiny portraits of my ancestors and descendants, passing the wealth of music through the years. I draw myself rocking an infant. Lullabies have been important in my tiny log cabin in the snowy mountains.

I lie still on my bed, travelling through my life, remembering music in all of the places I have lived, within my family of origin, through my own childbearing years, knitting together groups, telling stories on stage, building community, carrying traditions, lifting the spirits, sharing emotions, wrapping experiences, preserving culture.

It is a real turning point in my life. When I see Jon Samson, I see myself better. I feel better about who I am. I feel like what I have to offer the world has value. I feel oriented to my own Self and not outcast and isolated and like I have to say, "Look at ME everybody!" Or else suffer in solitude.

↖↑↗

What Happened Next?

Jon Samson began to record his co-creative compositions. He sent me digital files, asking for my input. He gave me copies of his recordings.

I made him a small quilt with pictures illustrating some of his songs. We continued to encourage each other by email and phone calls.

I used some of his music in my dance classes, and shared his songs when I volunteered in public school classrooms.

I felt like I had 'The Midas Touch' and every project I worked on turned to gold. Creativity was easy. My attitude was bright.

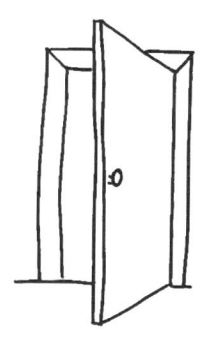

Chapter 8
Tuesday, February 12, 2008

Vulnerability is not weakness.
Vulnerability is about showing up and being seen.
It's tough to do that when
we're terrified about what people might see or think.
Vulnerability is the birthplace
of innovation, creativity and change.
—Dr. Brené Brown

↘↓↙

"I am so glad we are doing this together!" I have just pulled into the Aboriginal Friendship Centre in Clearwater, where Cheryl is just turning the key in the lock.

"Need a hand?" She already has a basket full of home baking and the textbook we need today. Swiftly, she begins to brew the coffee and lay out the refreshments.

"I got it!" I call back. I unload my easel with the flip-chart diagrams ready for the class. "Isn't it great how this seminar is so well organized?" I am setting out eleven chairs in a semi-circle.

It's like old times to be volunteering on a project with Cheryl again. Since she moved to Clearwater, she has been active in just about every non-profit society, club and annual event in town. In 2002, she was honoured for her volunteer efforts with the Queen's Jubilee Award.

Now that I have my driver's license and I bartered for my own car, I have been participating in groups much more often than ever before. It's great!

Nine ladies will join us today for the second of six sessions prepared by the University of Victoria Centre on Aging.[15] At first I didn't see why Cheryl had invited me to go to Kamloops with her for the two-day training. But as soon as I looked over the textbook and leader's manual, I became fully interested. 'Living a Healthy Life with Chronic Conditions' is the textbook, packed with practical, encouraging, clearly explained self-management tasks for people living with chronic conditions.

Fortunately, I do not suffer from any medical conditions, however, depression is also on the list. And, boy-oh-boy, I have had my turn with that!

Although each condition has different treatments, there are many concerns and problems that people living with chronic conditions have in common. It is the belief of this organization that by sharing information and brainstorming for ideas, participants will realize that developing a sense of connection is more healthy than feeling alone. As each individual prepares a specific Action Plan every week, participants will be able to make deliberate choices about their own habits and maintain a much better level of health than if they rely only on pills and doctor's appointments.

Tuesday, February 12, 2008

Cheryl and I have divided the lesson so that we take turns leading, have the charts ready, can take dictation when it is time to brainstorm, and encourage each other in the leadership skills we learned in the training.

"Success leads to success, Cheryl!" I glance at the clock. The people will be arriving any minute.

"I am confident that I can do the next task!" Cheryl smiles back. We learned these mini pep talks in the training seminar.

After greeting each other and as the room quiets, we begin by sharing. "How did you do with your 'Action Plan' from last week?" Leaders model the technique, then one-by-one each participant responds.

"My Action Plan," Cheryl begins, "was that I would (a) walk around the block (b) after my husband leaves for work (c) every weekday morning. (d) Between 0 and 10, I was '9' confident that I would succeed... And I did!"

Others chose a variety of specific goals, pledged to do them at a specific time of day, for a specific duration, and stated their confidence level. Today each person reported on their success. It is the second week, so it is the first time we have done this part of the weekly program. I see quite a few smiles and a few reluctant faces.

As expected in any group, there is an 'Eeyore.' Gloomy and dissatisfied, she is expecting us to 'fix' her problems. "I couldn't do my Action Plan because the phone kept ringing and interrupting me all week."

I glance at my notes in the margin of the leader's manual. There is a way to handle this situation. "May we use this as an example of problem solving?" I ask permission, get a nod, and the group brainstorms for ideas. "Has anyone else ever had a similar problem?" Leaders aren't expected to delve into 'why' or give suggestions. We open the way for members of the group to come up with their own solutions.

Brainstorming is tricky. We write the responses down just as they are stated, without comment or editing. This is not the time for discussion. When they seem to be finished, I ask the original gloomy person, "Do you see any strategies which you might try? Which one? Can that be part of your Action Plan for this next week? Would you be willing to report the results when you come next time?"

In fact, the lesson this week is exactly this rotation of problem solving. Identify the problem. List ideas. Select one. Assess the results. Make a substitution or alternative, or seek additional resources. And, sometimes, it is realistic to accept that the problem is not solvable right now.

Cheryl reviews, reading what the group collected on the flip-chart pages. "Last week we brainstormed, listing ideas on the topic of 'How my chronic condition affects my daily life.' Your observations included: I am in pain. I feel tired, grumpy, angry, scared, alone, depressed. I have too much sleep, no sleep, constipation, heart pounding, weight gain. It impacts my relationships because I can only do limited activities so I unexpectedly have to cancel future plans. I've lost some friends because they see me as if I am a yo-yo with ups and downs. Life is on and off. I've experienced economic loss such as sick days, cost of treatment, and cost of gas to get to appointments and treatments." Cheryl reads aloud, moving her hand across the page so the group can follow along.

"When a new problem is discovered or I have changes in medication or one condition leads to another, the frustration begins all over again. I can't walk, see, talk, drive, write or hear as well as I used to. It's frustrating in so many ways, such as memory loss and disappointing to not meet other people's expectations. It's time consuming to travel to the doctor and wait for appointments. Changing to a new doctor is also stressful."

Turning to the next page, it was my turn to continue reading.

"To introduce the concept of this course, we identified the main Self-Management Tasks:

1) take care of your own health problem
2) carry out normal activities
3) manage emotional changes"

The leader's manual is easy for me to follow. "Another thing we did last week was to agreed on the participants' responsibilities. Come to every session. Ask questions. Respect confidentiality. Do your homework. Be patient with yourself because it takes at least two weeks for new changes to make a difference. Make a weekly Action Plan. Choose a telephone buddy."

So far so good. Now I introduce today's new material.

"We will refer to this chart again and again," I point to each label around a large circle I drew on the flip-chart. "This is called The Symptom Cycle and reminds us of experiences we may have in common, although our chronic conditions and treatments differ. There are the Symptoms of the Disease, Tense Muscles, Stress also called Anxiety, Feelings of Anger or Frustration or Fear, Depression, and Fatigue."

This course will be repeating this sequence during each session over six weeks. Report on the success and challenges of the Action Plan from the previous week. Introduction of a new topic. Group brainstorming to suggest alternatives. Explain more information. Make a new Action Plan.

↘↓↙

"That went well!" I smile and begin to put the chairs away. Leaders always debrief after each session. Positive communication is part of the success of the program. "I am glad we plan ahead to divide the tasks." Cheryl and I have worked on so many volunteer projects together, we are a team and can move and think at the same time.

"You handled that interruption very well," Cheryl comments while washing the tea cups. "I was going to 'fix it' by offering my own suggestions and you remembered to 'throw the monkey back' by letting the whole group provide ideas."

"I am just amazed how good *I* feel after each session." I pause so I can find words to describe a new sensation. "I feel like the gloomy February limitations that always feel like a closed door has suddenly swung wide open to realize the potential of fresh, new possibilities!"

↘↓↙

Only a moment has passed, but, for me, a new chapter has begun.

My mind is already assimilating all that I learned today. I didn't realize how much I have in common with so many other people.

"What is your Action Plan this week?" Cheryl's eyes are twinkling at me. She likes to challenge me. She stimulates excellence in herself and everyone she is in contact with.

"Oooo, well, let me see." I open my Day Book. There are scribbles on every page. "I have so many ways to earn money now! I have a seminar with homeschooling families this afternoon. I have Home Visits on Wednesday, volunteer with 'Roots of Empathy' on Thursday, and go up to Blue River to lead 'Mother Goose' on Friday. On Saturday and Sunday I have to look after my house, prepare food for the week, and make a lot of phone calls to set up the Cub Scout banquet and the 'Home Organization Workshop' next week. Monday I teach 'Making

Connections, Making Dance.' And then it's Tuesday again and we are back here!"

I know Cheryl's schedule is just as packed. I am so glad I have a car, an income and so many intertwined activities. "I think my Action Plan will be this: On Saturday and Sunday I will prepare healthy suppers for Kevin and I as well as the foods I need to carry with me on the days I am away from home. That way I will be neither hungry and grumpy, nor grabbing chocolate bars and junk food. Bran muffins, soups, raw veggies, fruit, that should do it. And I am a '10' for confidence that I will get this Action Plan done successfully."

"I'm sure you will," she gives me a big hug. "See you next week," Cheryl is off to go to her next project.

↘↓↙

Now I get to go do my favourite thing: provide an 'edu-play' project for homeschooling families with young children. Our theme is 'Peoples of the North.' Today we will use boats made of milk cartons to develop trade between Europe and Canada. Lincoln Logs, furs, sparkly stones, corn and fish are exported from Canada. Textiles, pots and pans, glassware and other manufactured goods are brought into Canada. The children are small. The country is big. The parents are grateful. My creativity flows. My heart is happy.

↘↓↙

What Happened Next?
By the end of the Chronic Disease Self-Management course, participants had shared many experiences and the leaders had complied and preserved quite a lot of information by writing on the flip-chart pages.

Ideas to practice relaxation of tense muscles included: distraction, self-talk, guided imagery, visualization, prayer or meditation.

We learned that the causes of fatigue might be: the disease, inactivity, poor nutrition, insufficient rest, stress/tension, depression, medication side effects.

Nutrition was an interesting topic. First we came up with a list of benefits of eating healthy foods:

It can prevent side effects of medications. You have more energy. Emotions are more in balance. Body runs better. You don't gain weight.

Then we tackled the challenges. We brainstormed for things that prevent you from eating healthy: Not having proper foods in fridge. Don't go shopping when you're hungry. Cooking for one person. Sense of taste not as clear at it used to be, less pleasure and more wanting goodies. Lower income and food is more expensive.

It was very encouraging to think of solutions to address these problems: Buy in bulk, shop sales, stick to basics, make a list, buy fresh, buy at Farmer's Market, grow a garden or trade with someone who does, use your crock pot, prepare your own food by freezing, do home canning, make home baking.

To counteract inactivity we learned that there are three kinds of exercise: flexibility, strength and aerobic. A sensible way to look at improving your own fitness routine is to remember this word: FIT.

F is for frequency, I is for intensity. T is for time. You can improve by increasing each or all of these.

To help us manage our emotional changes we practiced communication skills. Can you identify your feelings? One way to express them is by saying, "When this happens, I feel ___." We practiced listening attentively and asking for clarification.

Tuesday, February 12, 2008

Communication was also an important topic: when we learn about medications, doctor visits and including our family in medical and end-of-life decisions.

We covered the role of positive and negative self-talk and the option of using distraction as a short term method of governing our emotions.

↘↓↙

What I was most interested in was the brainstorming about depression, something we all seemed to share.

Here is the list we collected when we brainstormed about the symptoms of depression.

- Loss of self-image, low self-esteem
- How am I going to deal with this?
- Overwhelmed, inability to make decisions
- Daily activities feel too hard
- Can't sleep, too much sleep
- Wake in the middle of the night
- Mind going too fast
- Confused, can't sort priorities
- 'I have to get out of here'
- Anger, arguments, see negative all the time
- Loose interests in normal activities, hobbies, sex
- Lack of self-care
- Loneliness, unhappy, cry
- Tired, can't get going
- Frequent accidents, clumsy,
- Suicidal thoughts
- Isolate yourself
- Crutch: food, alcohol, drugs

Too much time on TV, internet
Everything seems like a monotonous task

I have experienced many of these upsetting feelings. I had no idea anyone else felt any of these things.

Because of this experience, I realize that chronic depression is real. I'm not making it up or just laying around feeling sorry for myself and complaining. I am not stupid. But I can take positive steps towards self-management. I will never think "I am so alone" when and if I ever notice the heavy, gloomy feelings returning. And I will have tools to use to address the situation myself, ask for support from friends and family or get medical intervention.

Physically, I can go outdoors and get some fresh air and sunshine, engage in a physical activity or fitness routine. I can renew my commitment to avoid foods that throw me out of balance. I can fast to get rid of toxins and choose nourishing foods. I can be sure that I am taking medication properly.

Mentally, I can monitor my self-talk, take time with a pleasant hobby to benefit from colour or music, focus on a positive attitude, make commitments, look ahead, make a change.

Socially, I can interact with other people, or do something to help another person, or take care of living things to feel needed such as a garden, houseplants or pets.

Spiritually, I can collect poems, posters, quotations and songs that are up-lifting, wholesome and bring comfort.

If I am not improving with this self-management, I can phone to make a doctor or counselling appointment, ask for information, and be sure I have the facts to make good decisions for myself.

Tuesday, February 12, 2008

↘↓↙

I have kept my leader's manual, my notes and those flip-charts. I don't even have to read them. Just seeing them makes me feel strong.

It's normal to have problems. And there are various ways to solve them.

I feel like I have a toolbox. And I know how to use it.

I am not lost in a swampy jungle. I have options.

Chapter 8
Thursday, March 11, 2010

Imagination
is more important
than knowledge.
—*Albert Einstein*

↖↑↗

I loved being in Brownies. Eight years old, Third Grade, Colorado, new house, new baby sister, it is a time in my childhood that I remember clearly. We met on Wednesdays after school. Because I wasn't going home, I took a different yellow school bus from the three-room elementary school in the little town of Cascade to the meeting place at the Church in the Wildwood in Green Mountain Falls, Colorado.

I loved my uniform. Every week, I would wear it to school: the light brown dress that Mother would iron for me, the brown elastic belt with the Brownie belt buckle, brown knee socks, the little brown felt tam hat. I still have my pin.

I loved the opening and closing ritual. Begin by standing straight and tall, holding up two fingers and recite in unison the Brownie Promise.

*On my honour I will try
to do my duty to God and my country,
to help other people every day,
especially those at home.*

End with the Brownie circle. Standing, each girl crosses her arms right over left, holding hands with the Brownies on either side. Together we sing.

*Day is done, gone the sun,
from the lake, from the hills, from the sky.
All is well, safely rest, God is nigh.*

For a moment, there is silence. Each Brownie, one-by-one, feels a squeeze on her left hand, pauses to make a private prayer or intention, indicates when she is finished by pointing her right foot into the centre of the circle, then passing the squeeze with her right hand to the next Brownie. When the squeeze has been passed all the way around the circle, still holding hands, with a step, and a twist, and a turn, we un-cross our arms and facing outward, we are dismissed... being careful not to step back into or across the Brownie Ring.

I loved the songs.

*When 'ere you make a promise,
consider well its importance.
And when made,
engrave it upon your heart.*

I loved the Rounds. This was my first experience with singing in harmony.

Make new friends but keep the old.
One is silver and the other gold.

I loved the rotation of the year: Enrollment in the fall. Christmas songs and crafts. Thinking Day on February 22 with crafts, songs, cultural traditions and foods from around the world. Selling cookies in the spring: peanut butter, mint chocolate, vanilla and chocolate creme.

I loved my first attempts at volunteering. Inviting new girls to come to meetings in the fall. 'Trick-or-Treat for UNICEF' in October. Singing carols for the seniors at Christmastime. Litter chase in the spring. The Memorial Day Parade in May. 'Bridging' at the end of the school year, when the older girls left Brownies and entered Girl Scouts.

I loved the sense of belonging. The following year, when I joined the Girl Scouts, the Promise and Laws included this phrase, 'A Girl Scout is a friend to all and a sister to every other Girl Scout.' I was a child, but I knew that I was a small participant in a world-wide organization of girls and women, all of them making the same Promise, all of them learning, all of them striving towards high ideals, all of them challenging themselves to make the world a better place to be.

↖↑↗

I loved it all so much that when the photographer came for School Picture Day, I asked my Mother for permission to wear my Brownie uniform. The night before, she tied my hair in rags to curl it. Maybe I was humming this song in my head while the camera focused on my smiling face.[16]

I have something in my pocket
that belongs across my face.
I keep it very close to me
in a most convenient place.
I'm sure you'd never guess it
if you guessed a long long while.
So I'll take it out and put it on.
It's a great big Brownie smile.

If I could pass on one part of my childhood to my own children, if I could do one volunteer project with children when I grow up, I would want to recreate this marvellous experience.

As an adult, even when I have been 'down in the dumps,' feeling disconnected, struggling with self-doubt, feeling darkness all around me, heavy with immobilizing depression, lost on my Faith Journey, the Brownie Promise and Girl Scout Laws have kept me on track.

↖↑↗

In 1988, when Elise was in Grade Three, she went to school in Blue River, walked to the meeting place and stayed overnight so she could attend Brownies. The following year, I became the leader, 'Brown Owl.' I invited the Blue River Brownies to come to Avola on the school bus for meetings. Eagerly, I shared the customs and songs, seasonal activities and creative projects. It was interesting to adapt to some up-dated ideas and the Canadian way to do things.

Elise's Canadian uniform was a darker brown, long sleeved dress, which I lovingly ironed. I so wanted to keep it, to hold onto this precious moment in a tangible way, but the custom was to pass the dresses along to future Brownies, so I did. Canadians said, 'Girl Guides' instead of 'Girl Scouts.' Canadian kerchiefs featured maple leaves. The Canadian Promise was a little different, too. I had to remember to pledge 'to do my duty to God, *the Queen* and my country.' Canadian girls knew that Queen Elizabeth herself was a sister in Guiding.

First thing, I showed the girls how to make a little felt pouch they could button to their uniform so they would always remember to bring their 'Brownie Gold' weekly dues of 25¢.

Last thing, before summer break, we had an indoor overnight camp. I made a pretend campfire with small logs and yellow and orange tissue paper and a flashlight. The girls spread out their bedding around it, like spokes of a wheel. I dreaded late-night shenanigans, so when I tucked the girls into their sleeping bags, I started to serenade them with quiet songs accompanied on my guitar. Within three songs, the room was silent.

↖↑↗

I loved the scope and variety of activities offered to the girls including: Home, Community, World and the Outdoors. Badges for Arts and Crafts and Handwork (art appreciation, bead-work, crafts, dance, knitting, music, photography, puppets, singing, making toys, weaving, writing), Sports and Fitness (athlete, baton twirling, cyclist, gymnast, horse riding, skating, snowshoeing, swimming, team sports), Health and Hospitality and Domestic Skills (baker, cook, holidays, hostess, housekeeping, neighbour, pets), Outdoor Skills (astronomer, explorer, birds and animals, camping skills, gardener, native lore, observer, space, winter adventure).

Although I have always been a little jealous of child movie stars, musicians, and sports champions, I rejected the idea of focusing on one skill for many hours, over many years to the exclusion of developing a broader repertoire. In the Girl

Guide program, with a little time and effort, a young girl could explore and appreciate a wide variety of topics and sample many things, developing lifelong interests.

↖↑↗

After 2004, when all of our children left home, I was at a loss. No more homeschooling. No more chores and outings. No more cheery children eager to help with preparations for seasonal celebrations. For so many years, so much of every one of my days had been focused on my children's needs and activities. What else holds any interest for me? How shall I spend my time? What do I have to give? Who, where and what could I teach? What projects are worth my time to volunteer? The school in Avola had been closed since 1984, twenty years ago. All of the children who used to live here are grown and gone. If I wanted to volunteer with children, I would have to go 25 miles north to Blue River or 45 miles south to Clearwater.

Not fully understanding how to smoothly make the transition to 'The Empty Nest,' continually searching through memories, wondering what to say or do to improve the situation, tired and dreary, I consulted an art therapist. When she suggested I work on a timeline as a way to see my own life, I discovered another wonderful thing about Brownies... and about my 'Self.'

As a child my biggest and happiest influences were these seven things: living in the mountains of Colorado, experiencing Brownies and Girl Scouts, reading all of Laura Ingalls Wilder's 'Little House' books, learning about Helen Keller and her teacher, Annie Sullivan, having a baby sister, developing creative expression in dance classes, and going to Sunday School.

As a Mother, I had deliberately brought these same seven treasures to our children. Kevin and I decided to raise our

Thursday, March 11, 2010

family living in the mountains. I became a Brownie leader so that Elise could have this experience. When the time was right, I read the 'Little House' books aloud. We watched 'The Miracle Worker' movie about Helen Keller and Annie Sullivan. I included Elise and Michael in caring for the new babies as they joined our family. I led dance classes and Sunday School at home and in Avola.

As I continued to draw on my timeline, I could see that these seven treasures had played a significant role in my life twice. First, they were given to me during my own childhood. Second, I gave them to my own children. I also discovered that they are not all gone! They are still important to me! My happiness does not only depend on whether or not my own children are here to participate in these things with me.

There could be a third time! Surely I can continue to find ways to participate in these seven activities even as I grow older?

This realization is what led to the present. A year ago, I offered to play guitar and be a song leader for a Girl Guide camp. While I was there, I learned that a Brownie leader was needed 45 miles away in Clearwater. I jumped right in.

Remembering how my Mother and Aunt Barbara were my leaders, I began to experience the teamwork of Guiding. I met the other leaders for Sparks, Brownies, Guides and Pathfinders. Kim and Heather, Katrina and Pearl, Cindy and Jean, Mary and Judy, Jane and Kris, Sandi and Kay are such marvellous women, and we are all sisters! I most often attended their evening meetings through the use of my speaker phone.

This year, leading the Brownies, I have been paired with Jean Nelson, who is also the District Commissioner. A woman in her 70s, with over 30 years' experience with Girl Guides, she also has any number of other connections within the community.

Jean Nelson is a treasure trove of knowledge who has collected a warehouse of materials, supplies and equipment. A mentor offering depths of wisdom from decades of experience she has been an example to generations of girls and women. A lifelong learner she continuously challenges herself, reaching towards excellence in each of her many and increasing interests. She is a voice to harken to through public speaking and writing and is woven throughout the community through service groups, clubs, event planning and the government of organizations. A First Aider, a naturalist, a hostess, an artist in her garden and kitchen, she is practical and athletic, overflowing with stamina. A true teacher, she passes knowledge on to others, encouraging each person, until they can hike, ski, swim, canoe, tie knots, travel and continue to strive for excellence alone, or better yet, become a Guide Leader!

She is the Brown Owl, and she likes outdoor physical activities and camping skills. I am the Tawny Owl, and I like singing, crafts, drama, storytelling and being cozy indoors. So the children will gain from both skill sets. We have fourteen girls aged seven to nine, from different backgrounds, many entering Brownies for the first time. Some are homeschooling and this is their big outing for the week, some in lower income or single parent families, some who have multiple after school music or sport activities, some new to town, some with four generations of extended family settled here. Every shining face and pair of sparkling eyes shows the girls are eager to participate.

It is a very special year. We are celebrating 100 years of Guiding in Canada: 1910-2010.

A letter introduces the parents to our 'Open Door' policy and welcomes their involvement, coming to watch their children as they learn, and inviting parents to take on the role as leader next year. The new uniforms have changed. Now Brownies wear navy blue pants, an orange t-shirt, and a blue and white maple leaf scarf.

Learning the ceremonies, songs, games, crafts and badge choices occupy the first few meetings. October brings World Hunger Day and donations to the local Food Bank. A sleepover weekend at Brown Owl's house is fun for all. My experience preparing curriculum for homeschooling comes in handy when I construct a booklet for each girl to collect information about Canada 100 years ago. What kind of kitchen, cars, music, entertainment, games, toys, sports, school, Girl Guide uniforms, fashion, and telephones did people have back then?

Next comes a Halloween party. Then a Remembrance Day project on the theme of 'Peace,' followed by a dress-up day considering career options, and finally, the traditional Christmas carolling at the retirement home, including delivery of home-baked cookies.

'Key to my Community' and 'All About Canada' and 'Family Heritage' badges are nearly complete.

The 'Key to Active Living' badge we link to the 2010 Winter Olympics, celebrated in Vancouver! The girls have learned the meaning of the Olympic Rings and participated in the ceremony at the high school when the Olympic Torch passed through Clearwater. The Brownies also made national flags to wave at our mini opening ceremony and silly races we planned during the wintertime meetings.

February 22 is set aside as 'World Thinking Day.' Every year Guides and Scouts around the world remember their founders, Lord and Lady Baden-Powel. This year, we made paper dolls each with a uniform from other countries.

March is cookie selling month! Wear your uniform. Go in pairs. Aim to sell three cases.

Later, we will plant trees in a local park.

Soon it will be time to plan the year-end event at a local resort. Badges will be presented. Sparks will advance to Brownies, and Brownies to Guides, and Guides to Pathfinders.

Awards and words of thanks to our volunteers will all be presided over by the international Girl Guide flag, a symbol of unity, ideals and world peace. After the potluck dinner, the plan is to take the girls on a paddle-wheeler boat ride across Dutch Lake and around the island.

↖↑↗

Meanwhile, bigger plans for a summertime event have my attention today.

I am driving for two-and-a-half hours to the city of Kamloops for an 11:00am meeting with the regional Girl Guide Leaders. We are getting organized for a summer camp with girls from the surrounding area. 'The Sky's the Limit' is the theme for this Centennial Year, with an emphasis on encouraging the girls to reach for their highest potential. Recently, I have earned the reputation as a song leader, so I am very excited to participate in this wider world.

It's amazing. I have my own car! I can come and go any time I choose. I can participate in so many activities. My day-book is crammed with paid and volunteer work. I never would have dreamed that this chapter in my life would be so much fun, meeting interesting people, adding my skills to the groups, bringing enjoyment to others. It is all so wonderful.

I drive from the tiny village of Avola, curve alongside the river, pass through Clearwater and Barriere, to enter the busy traffic in the city of Kamloops.

The team planning the camp is meeting at Anne's house, up high on the sandy hills. After we settle in and make introductions, each committee head has updates to report on the venue, outings, food, camping arrangements, first aid tent, opening and closing ceremonies. One ambitious suggestion is to bring in a real hot air balloon or ask the local skydivers to demonstrate their skills!

Then it's my turn to share ideas for a singalong, and other ways music can be part of the three-day event. There has been some research done looking into a proposal to get a big name entertainer for the closing event.

"If 'The Sky's the Limit' is the theme you have chosen," I eagerly offer my suggestion, "and if that means we will be encouraging the girls to explore their own potential and strive for excellence, if we have a budget for an entertainer who can also give instruction, I know who I'd get. Jon Samson is a music therapist, song writer, recording artist and entertainer in Brooklyn, New York. I have been to Brooklyn. I have observed Jon working one-to-one, participated in his group events, heard his original music, and appreciate his positive message. I am astonished at the skill he has to bring children to express themselves through music. Truly, if you are looking for a musician with a message to match your theme, I would say that Jon Samson is it!"

↖↑↗

What Happened Next?
They all liked the idea!

I met Jon at the airport. He brought his ukulele. We rented drums. I brought my electric keyboard and guitar.

Throughout the three days, small groups of girls experienced challenges, rhythm, laughter, participation, all with Jon's special leadership in co-creative cooperation.

There it was. The answer to my questions when I first met Jon. 'Authentic.' That was the right word to describe his work as a music therapist.

After the camp, we came to Clearwater. Jon Samson entertained children for several events at the library and added leadership to my dance class. He also held a seminar for professionals who work with children. Best of all was Saturday's Farmer's Market. I had been volunteering at the elementary school to share his music. The students had made actions and dances for some of his songs. He gave us the tunes. We gave him the dances. The parents snapped pictures. *Nothing Rhymes with Orange*[17] was a big hit. *The Conductor* got everyone moving.

Last of all, this city boy came to our homestead to pick raspberries, dig potatoes and make a salad with greens from our garden. Kevin guided Jon on a mountain hike.

↖↑↗

It is a long way from the tiny town of Avola to the metropolis of NYC. I don't know if we will ever be in the same place at the same time again.

But, e-mail is one way to communicate.

E-mail from Jon:

You, Eleanor, I will call: 'Vitamin E!'
I am so glad I came to meet you and Kevin.
What a beautiful life you have chosen.

Peace ~ Jonathan Samson

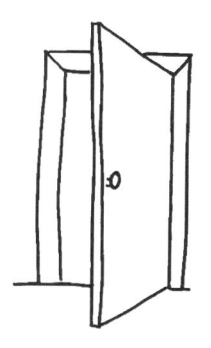

Chapter 9
Sunday, February 6, 2011

>Turn your face to the sunshine
>and you cannot see the shadow
>—Helen Keller

The five Sunday School children I teach in Blue River have a surprise for Father Sasges. They have made him birthday cards. After Mass, their mothers and other neighbours have planned a potluck supper and chocolate cake. 80 years old is a significant thing to celebrate. 54 years a priest! Each family pitched in a few dollars to buy a gift. It is a blue fleece blanket decorated with a soaring eagle. I have embroidered these four verses around the four outside edges.

>I bore you up on eagles' wings.
>Exodus 19:4

Like an eagle that stirs up its nest...
and bears the young on its wings...
so the Lord alone shall lead them...
Deuteronomy 32:11

Too wonderful for me...
is the way of an eagle in the sky...
Proverbs 30:18-19

They who wait on the Lord
shall renew their strength,
they shall mount up with wings
like eagles.
Isaiah 40:31

    Accepting the greetings, gift, meal and affection, Father Emil Sasges hangs the blanket up like a banner on the wall in the room where we hold nondenominational Sunday School and Catholic Mass during the frigid winter months when the tiny church, Our Lady of the Snows, is too chilly to heat.

↘↓↙

This meeting room has become my favourite place to be. Warm from the wood stove down in the basement, welcoming with the soft blue couch where Father invites people to sit and share their questions and concerns, multi-purpose with tables and chairs, a piano, book shelf, the kitchen and washroom down the hall. Huge Christmas cactus bloom midwinter and geraniums fill the window sills with red during the summer. Framed portraits of the Pope, the Bishop, and our Priest, smile down on whoever comes here.

Sunday, February 6, 2011

In this meeting room two years ago I asked a zillion questions. In this meeting room one year ago I made my first Confession, received my First Communion, and at age 52, entered the Catholic Church.

I am not alone on Sundays anymore. Even if I cannot attend, I know that Mass is celebrated every day in every time zone around the world. I am not alone during Christian holidays anymore. Even without extended family, I know that I join millions of others as the cycle of the Liturgical Year brings Advent, Christmas, Epiphany, Lent, Holy Week, Easter, Pentecost, saints days, and Marian feasts. I am not alone anymore as I prepare lessons for the children. I am part of an oral tradition that reaches back to most ancient times, relaying these sacred stories 'that you shall tell the next generation.'

At first, I was disinclined to participate at all, although I found Father Sasges to be so kind and genuine, wise and patient. But, still! The Catholic Church? How medieval it all seemed: statues, robes, ritual, candles, processions, ancient texts, names of people, and places, and customs passed down for centuries.

At first, although I was very reluctant, I decided to read the entire Catechism which explains the teachings of the Church in a 700 page book!

At first, each time Father and I began a new topic in our discussion, I felt cynical. Angels? Really? Mary? Why? Does God Almighty actually care about the minutia of my life?

Maybe I was allowing one person to have too much influence on me? I watched daily Mass on TV, listened to more than a dozen priests, took notes and used the internet to research. I kept Kevin up-to-date on all of the conversations I had with Father Sasges. I compared Catholic teaching with the Seer-Church doctrine that I was raised with. The Seer speaks harshly of the 'Papists,' but then, he was writing in the early to mid-1700s. Church history in Europe was not always pleasant.

Then I listened to an eight hour seminar in CDs called 'The Great Adventure, A Journey Through the Bible,' by Jeff Cavins. The continuity of the Bible was laid out in plain English. I came to see that the whole history of the human race has been one, long story of salvation history. And, it is also one tiny story. Each person has a choice. Turn towards, or turn away from the God of all. I can say 'Yes' and trust God's order, guidance and Word. Or I can say, 'No, thanks. I can do this by myself,' and live in whatever way seems best to me at the time. Individually and altogether, the Bible tells the story of what we all do.

Some parts of the Bible record the 'Yes.' Some parts of the Bible record the 'No.' I am part of this story. I say 'Yes' and 'No,' too. But, the Good News is, the 'No' is not irreversible. Individuals, tribes, whole nations turned away to follow false ideas. More than once. But, when Jesus spoke, even as He took His last breath on the Cross, He shared the central message from God, "Father, forgive them, they know not what they do." That includes me, too. I cannot undo my wrongs. I cannot be 'good enough.' I cannot earn, or deserve, or wash myself clean enough to be with God. Heaven is a gift. Grace. I can only accept the cleansing of forgiveness, and bow in awe.

I also read several of Scott Hahn's books.[18] Previously a Protestant Bible scholar, he had the same reservations I did as he became ever more interested in and eventually converted to the Catholic Church.

↘↓↙

Today, during Father Sasges' birthday party, I keep taking pictures, trying to hold on to this sense of belonging. Familiar voices, smiling faces, comfortable conversation, the birthday guest of honour, the children, the elderly. In this cozy meeting room surrounded by wilderness mountains and heaps of snow, we are a tiny part of this wider community: the Church.

↘↓↙

One daily custom I now engage in gives me the clearest confirmation that I have made a good decision to join the Catholic Church.

Last February, a few weeks after I entered the Church, Father Sasges gave me a thick red prayer book and showed me how to use it. The cycle of the day, the cycle of the year, the consecration of time is what is offered through this discipline. Immediately I felt that precious sense of connection. As I began to read, I began to realize that the Father Almighty, who is apart from time and space, enters time and space through the Son, then sends the Holy Spirit to us when we open our hearts, allow stillness and silence, follow the path of believers before us, listen to the Word, and bear fruit in our daily tasks when we love and serve Him and our neighbour.

'Christian Prayer' is printed in gold letters on the front. This book is also called 'The Breviary' or 'Liturgy of the Hours.' There are 2078 pages of Psalms and responses, prayers and hymns, Biblical readings and an index. At the back there are dates and biographical notes to remember the saints and short sermons preserved from the writings of the earliest Church Fathers. Together with the Bible and Catechism, I have an entire library at my fingertips!

Overwhelmed and somewhat confused, I decided to start at the beginning of the Breviary. Although it was February, the first 240 pages mark the time from Advent (four weeks before Christmas) through Christmas, to January 2nd (when the Church celebrates the baptism of Jesus).

And this is when I experience the benefit of participating in this daily prayer custom. My usual wintertime depression can not co-exist with the red book in my hands. I wake at 5:00am, help Kevin prepare to leave for work at 6:00am, and open the Breviary to find today's reading.

As I sit, wrapped in layers of woollen blankets, watching the winter sky slowly turn from night to blue-dawn, these words of these Responses seem to nourish me deep inside.

> Your light will come...
> the Lord will dawn on you in radiant beauty...
>
> Let your face shine upon us...
>
> Dispel our darkness
> with the light of your presence...
>
> Father, creator of unfailing light,
> give that same light to those who call on you...
>
> May those you have called
> walk in the splendour of the new light...

Again and again, the Scripture quotations refer to 'Light.'

> The night is far spent...
> The day draws near.
> Romans 13
>
> Dismiss all anxiety...
> Present your needs to God.
> Philippians 4

Sunday, February 6, 2011

I am the Lord there is no other,
I form the light and create darkness.
Isaiah 45

I have been reading the Psalms since I was a teenager, but now, the light seems to be shining up right off the pages into my eyes, mind and heart.

From the rising of the sun to its setting,
praised be the name of the Lord.
Psalm 113

O God, rise above the heavens;
may your glory shine on earth!
Psalm 57

I rise before the dawn...
I hope in your word.
Psalm 119

I will bless the Lord who gives me counsel,
who even in the night directs my heart.
Psalm 16

Send forth your light and truth;
let these be my guide.
Psalm 43

These Refrains are recited between the Psalms.

The Lord is coming...
the day will dawn with a wonderful light...

The Lord will come with mighty power;
all mortal eyes shall see him.

O Radiant Dawn,
splendour of eternal light,
sun of justice,
shine on those who dwell in darkness...

The Prayers are overflowing with images of brightness and my heart opens to receive these beams.

Increase our longing for Christ...
that the dawn of His coming may find us...
welcoming the light...

Father in heaven,
our hearts desire the warmth of your love
and our minds are searching
for the light of your Word...

Christ the Lord, Son of the living God,
light from light, lead us into light...

Father in heaven,
the day draws near when the glory of your Son
will make radiant the night of the waiting world...

Lord,
let your glory dawn to take away our darkness.
May we be revealed as the children of light...

O Rising Sun that never sets..
come and shine on those who dwell in darkness...

Your law is light to my eyes...

Enkindle our hearts with the flame of your love...

May the light of faith shine in our actions...

Then I came to this Prayer to read on Christmas Day:

Almighty God and Father of Light,
a child is born for us and a son is given to us.
Your eternal Word leaped down from heaven
in the silent watches of the night,
and now your Church is filled with wonder
at the nearness of her God.
Open our hearts to receive His life
and increase our vision with the rising of dawn,
that our lives may be filled
with His glory and His peace,
who lives and reigns for ever and ever.

The ritual, prayers, postures, continuity of the liturgical year, songs both familiar and new, all compound in such a significant way. I feel energy flowing during the time of year when I have previously been so lethargic, and heavy, and dull of mind.

↘↓↙

The next time I went to town, I decided to ask the pharmacist about it.

"Can a happy prayer life make serotonin in your head?" I wondered.

"You bettcha!" she answered right away.

"I have not been taking the antidepressants this winter," I confided, "and I feel great!"

↘↓↙

The next Sunday, the weather closed in and I could not drive up over the Messiter Summit to Blue River to attend Mass. Disappointed, but turning immediately to the red Breviary, blue Catechism and Kevin's brown leather Bible, I spent the same hour in worship by myself. I was almost expecting the dreary isolation to press down on my heart. Most likely tears, or anger, or self-pity would be my companion for the afternoon. I was surprised by something very different.

My experience of the Lord's guidance was so specific that I sent Father Sasges this email.

> Father, Mentor, Friend and Guide,
>
> Here it is, the second Sunday in February, and there has been not a shadow or flicker of the depression that has so often kept me trapped. Kevin can see it and knows it is true. I have repeatedly told him that I am so sorry that I have been so hard to take and also how amazed I am that he has been so steady through it all.
>
> Here is a specific example of me seeing how I am hurtful and how the Lord is showing me things:
>
> Yesterday I phoned a high school girl friend (Kevin's friend, too, and he heard my conversation) in Pennsylvania because I just got her Christmas letter. She asked me if I like living in Avola. I said, "No, I don't like it here. There are no children left. There are no wise grannies left. I go

Sunday, February 6, 2011

other places to do the things I love to do. I come home
to look after my property and house and husband.
I make a big pot of soup so he will have supper for a few
days and then I go out to have more fun with people."

Kevin was grumpy that I said that. It always
hurts him when I say that to people.

So, while I was marking my Bible last night, as I flipped
the pages. Suddenly this passage grabbed my eyes:

Isaiah 45:9-12
Does the clay pot dare to argue with its maker?
Does the clay ask the potter what he is doing?
Does the pot complain that its maker has no skill?
Does anyone dare to say to his parents, "Why did you make
me like this?"
The LORD, the holy God of Israel, the one who shapes the
future says:
"You have no right to question me about my children or tell
me what I ought to do!
I am the one who made the earth and created mankind to
live there.
By my power I stretched out the heavens;
I control the sun, moon and stars."

So: THAT was a little bit of a scolding!
I asked the Lord for this lifestyle and now I am
complaining about what He gave me!

So, although I did not attend Mass today, I am having
a rather direct experience with the Lord ! ! !

I am so glad you are willing to listen to a fellow traveller on the Journey,
Eleanor

↘↓↙

Father Sasges' birthday dinner and cake were delicious. I stayed to tidy up and help the hostess with the dishes. Because of the snowy, dark, highway miles, I stayed overnight with a friend who kindly shares her spare room with me every Sunday during the wintertime.

Before I fell asleep, I reach for the Breviary to read the nighttime Prayers.

"What can bring us happiness?"
many say.
Let the light of your face
shine on us, O Lord.
You have put into my heart
a greater joy than they have
from an abundance
of corn and new wine.
I will lie down in peace
and sleep comes at once
for you alone, Lord,
make me dwell in safety.
Psalm 4

↘↓↙

What Happened Next?
When you have a friend who is past 80 years old, you can be pretty sure that you will someday have to say, 'Good-bye.'

In August, 2014, the time came.[19] As funeral preparations were being made, it was discovered that Father Sasges had built his own coffin of beautiful, local, red cedar! Some kind of lining was needed. I offered to use the eagle blanket banner. Tears prevented me from singing the familiar hymn as hundreds of voices filled the Sacred Heart Cathedral in Kamloops.

And He will raise you up on eagles wings,
bare you with the breath of dawn,
make you to shine like the sun,
and hold you in the palm of His hand.[20]

Chapter 9
Ash Wednesday, March 9, 2011

> There are only two ways to live your life.
> One is as though nothing is a miracle.
> The other is as though everything is a miracle.
> —Albert Einstein

↖↑↗

The priest enters, wearing purple, the colour of repentance.

It is the first time I have ever experienced Ash Wednesday.

The palm branches from the previous Palm Sunday celebration have been burned. The ashes are collected in a shallow dish and mixed with oil. One-by-one participants step forward and allow the priest to make the sign of the Cross on their forehead while he speaks these words, "Repent and believe the Gospel." The recipient replies, "Amen."

It is a very solemn and somewhat mysterious Mass. Around the world and through the centuries for these 40 days before Easter, believers mark this time for self-examination, repentance, and penance, realizing their utter dependence on the gift of forgiveness that God offers without ceasing through the life, death and resurrection of Jesus Christ.

It is my turn. I notice the faint charred smell. I see the priest reach the black mixture up to my forehead. I feel the oily, yet gritty sensation as he makes the sign of the cross with his thumb. I hear the repeated message, "Repent and believe the Gospel." What layers of meaning are contained in these brief words?

'Amen' means, 'I believe. I agree. Yes.' This is the expected, ritual response. Do I believe? In a flash of a split second I preface my assent with a silent prayer "Lord, I believe, help thou my unbelief." Mark 9:24.

Then I speak aloud, "Amen."

↖↑↗

Adam and Eve were banished from the Garden. Noah and his family were the only survivors after 40 days and 40 nights of rain in the flood. After the Plagues and Passover in Egypt, the twelve Tribes of the Children of Israel wandered for 40 years in the wilderness. Jesus was tempted for 40 days before he began his public ministry. For the 40 days of Lent, we participate in this banishment, this storm, this Passover, this temptation, this agony, this isolation, this darkness.

For me, Mass is like time travel. People and stories from long ago become present. The turning points that ancient characters passed through are still realities in my life Journey today. I am one of the characters taking part in this story through my actions, decision making and life choices. Passing through times of darkness is real. Believers trust that the Lord will provide bright times again.

Ash Wednesday, March 9, 2011

'We are a Resurrection People.' We believe that no matter how heavily the darkness presses in, light will overcome. But, we are also 'A People of the Cross.' During Lent, we pause, look more intently at Jesus' life, teachings, purpose, example and suffering. We pause to seek the meaning of the Stations of the Cross. We pause to deliberately Fast. We pause to offer 'alms' as gifts of money, time or effort. We pause to increase time spent in prayer.

It is very meaningful to me that this dark part of the cycle is acknowledged. Morning, noon, evening, *night*. Spring, summer, fall, *winter*. Infancy, youth, adulthood, *old age*. Sprout, growth, harvest, *dormancy*. You cannot have one without having all.

I used to wonder about Lent. What does it matter to God if I 'give up chocolate?' It seems to me now that what matters is experiencing the 'longing' and the 'craving.' Do I long for time with my Father? Do I crave time with Jesus?

Another thing I am noticing as I enter this sacred season: Some things you can't 'know' by watching. You cannot know what it is like to be married if you live together. You cannot know what it is like to have a child by holding a baby who belongs to someone else. You cannot know about prayer, or the Sacraments of Baptism or Confession or any of these other sacramental rituals, if you stay on the outside looking in. You have to actually step inside and do them.

So, I am.

↖↑↗

When I arrive home after Mass, I still have most of the day before Kevin returns from work. How shall I focus my time?

I look at the outline I have made for teaching Catechism every Tuesday after school in the Clearwater Catholic Church.

I have thirteen children aged three to eleven. The older children meet with another teacher to prepare for Confirmation.

The Liturgical Year is ordered into three cycles. This is Year A. The Gospel readings are mostly from the book of Matthew. Year B features Mark. Year C focuses on Luke. Selections from John are interspersed as needed to convey Jesus' teachings throughout the year.

Back in September, I began my first year of teaching the Catholic children. Until now I have been teaching nondenominational Sunday School at home, in Avola, and recently in Blue River where no one seems to care exactly what I am teaching. Now I have to be very careful to submit to the authority of the priest, and cover the required material, and meet the expectations of the parents. I cannot use the textbooks for separate grades since I have such a wide range of ages. I am not ready to clearly convey Catholic teachings I am still somewhat unfamiliar with. So, this year I am only teaching the basic Bible stories.

From September to late November we covered well-known Old Testament stories: Creation, Adam and Eve, Cain and Abel, Noah's Ark, the Tower of Babel, Abraham, Isaac and Jacob, Joseph in Egypt, Moses and the Ten Commandments, David and Goliath.

Every lesson is designed to provide: information and a memory verse to strengthen the mind, a craft project and song to stimulate the heart, a moment of prayer to nourish the spirit and a skit, or snack, or task to include the physical senses.

Meanwhile, I have to keep my wits about me to govern this group. The two oldest girls, Anna and Haley tend to go off by themselves and chatter away. The teacher's children have to leave early to get to hockey practice. One boy arrives a little late. He is quite stand-offish. His parents recently split up and he's understandably upset. A girl the same age with the same situation is hungry for attention. Neither of them attend Mass with any regularity. Another family is very religious and the children know the prayers and customs better than I do. June and Daisy love to help the younger ones. Claire and Viva are best friends and encourage each other to do their best. The little boys like to sit together, but then interrupt with their playing, so I have to seat them boy-girl-boy-girl like my teachers used to do. Little Soren never stops moving. He's only three.

In November, I realized that the five Joyful Mysteries preserved by reciting the Rosary are exactly the content the children needed as we approached Christmas: The Annunciation, Mary visits Elizabeth, the Nativity. We learned how Mary and Joseph travelled to Bethlehem, where Jesus was born, the angels, shepherds and wise men and the flight to Egypt. Later we learned about the Presentation in the Temple, and when Jesus was twelve and spoke with the leaders in the Temple.

In January, I noticed that the Gospel readings for Year A would all be from Matthew. Combined with the Luminous Mysteries of the Rosary, I conveniently have curriculum all in order until the end of the school year.

The Sermon on the Mount (Matthew chapters 5, 6 and 7) provided nine weeks of lessons and nine memory verses: the Beatitudes, You are the light of the world, love your enemies, the Our Father, consider the lilies, seek ye first the kingdom of God, ask and it will be given to you, by their fruits ye shall know them, and the house built on the sand.

↖↑↗

As we are now approaching springtime, starting next week, we need to focus on Jesus as he nears Jerusalem: Palm Sunday, the Passover, the Last Supper, the Garden of Gethsemane, the trial, the Crucifixion and the burial of Jesus. For the first time in my life, I spend time pondering the Stations of the Cross.

Why did they kill Jesus? Why didn't He stop them? Did Jesus know what was going to happen? Children, adults, even the disciples asked similar questions. They are important to struggle with until a satisfactory answer is found. How can I bring these children an experience that will strengthen them on their Faith Journey?

At Christmastime, the children so much enjoyed decorating cardboard tube figures to act out the Nativity story. Moving the figures of Mary, Joseph, the Baby Jesus, angels, shepherds and wise men, while retelling the story seems to really help them retain the information while bringing a gladness to the heart. To continue this way of learning, I think we will make Roman soldiers, temple priests, disciples, the crowd and little palm branches to line the roadway for Jesus to travel on for Palm Sunday. A hollow piece of wood makes the tomb with a large stone over the opening to represent the solemn burial. The Sorrowful Mysteries of the Rosary concentrate on these painful events.

On Easter morning, the empty tomb, risen Lord and silk flowers will complete the scene. When we get to 'The Road to Emmaus' story later, some of the children's questions will be answered. Jesus relates which prophesies point to His coming, suffering, death and resurrection. The Glorious Mysteries of the Rosary will anchor these scenes in the memory of the children.

I am coming to see how the Apostles' Creed, Rosary and Liturgical Year are containers holding what is precious which parents and teachers have vowed to pass to the next generation.

What Happened Next?
April 21, 22, 23, 24, 2011

When I was 16, a few months after I met Kevin, I decided to mark the time from Holy Thursday until Easter Sunday morning with Fasting, quietness and reading the whole book of Matthew.

Since then, as a Sunday School teacher and at home with my own children, I pay attention to these days, holding them as a reverent pause to focus on the reality of the words, events, characters, sequences and meaning of all that happened. As a family we watch 'The Ten Commandments' to understand the Passover. There are other movies based on the New Testament or fictional characters such as 'Ben Hur.' Flannel board figures are useful to retell the stories. Even the youngest child can participate.

This year is different. I don't have to invent a ritual for myself. I can participate for the first time in the Holy Week Mass... if only I can get there. I have decided to take the Greyhound bus to Valemount, stay in a motel, and walk to church every day. This may be the only time in my life that I can do this.

Thursday

The bus pulls in right beside the motel at 4:30pm. Mass is at 7:00. I settle into my motel room, walk across the street to order my last meal before my Fast begins, and then walk to the Good Shepherd Catholic Church. Tonight we commemorate the Last Supper.

The church building was designed from a duplex blueprint, with variations Father Sasges suggested back in the late 1960s when he became the first resident priest. The priest's apartment is in the top right half of the building. The left half is one big room for the sanctuary. The basement is a large community gathering place and two small classrooms. The building is heated primarily with a wood stove in the basement.

The Book of Exodus is read, relating the story of the first Passover. I notice the parallels and prophecies within the meanings of this ancient feast. The People are 'saved by the blood of the lamb.' The male lamb is to be 'unblemished' and his bones are 'not to be broken.' Although written nearly fourteen centuries before Jesus was born, each of these phrases also apply to Jesus.

> How can I repay the Lord
> for His goodness to me?
> The cup of salvation I will raise
> and call upon the name of the Lord.
> Psalm 115

Again, the ancient text foreshadows this particular night.

Next is John chapter 13 describing in detail the sequence of events and teachings of Jesus at the Last Supper.

What is this? People are moving. The priest has a basin, a jug of water and a towel. Like Jesus with his disciples, the priest is washing the parishioners' feet. My heart beats fast. It is so meaningful to see this reenactment with my own eyes as this highly respected leader goes down on his knees to perform this act of service.

Communion is especially solemn. Passover is celebrated on the night of the first Sabbath after the first full moon after the spring equinox. This is the time of year. This is the time of day. This is the anniversary of the very night. These are the words that were spoken. This is the Gift that was given. "Take. Eat. This is my Body. Take. Drink. This is my Blood."

Judas, the Betrayer, has already left to convey his message to the authorities. Jesus leaves the upper room and goes out into the darkness of the Mount of Olives to pray for strength to accomplish what is to come next. Will the disciples stay awake? No. He is utterly alone.

The next part of the ritual is another first for me. The priest removes the consecrated Host from the Tabernacle. The red candle which is always lit to signify Christ's Presence is extinguished. In 'a place of repose,' the Host is silently adored. All statues and pictures are draped. The altar is bare. No candles are lit. No flowers. Through these customs we deliberately focus on this moment.

Jesus suffers.

↖↑↗

Friday

During the day, I stay in my room, reading the three books I brought with me.

'The Day Christ Died,' by Jim Bishop, published in 1957, dramatically narrates this day from the late night arrest, through the trial, interviews with officials, mocking, scourging, carrying the Cross, the last words, death and burial of Jesus. The setting in Jerusalem, character traits of the major players, responsibilities of the various levels of authority, Roman customs, Jewish Laws, Peter's denial, the sound of the cock crow, all come to life on these descriptive pages.

I pause to imagine, and return to read as the day goes by. It is all so dramatically described: the illegal trail by night, the disciples hiding in fear of capture, the High Priest ripping his garments and shouting "Blasphemer!" I can almost hear the rhythm of the marching Romans, their prisoner silent. I can almost see the blood running from each wound as the sharp shards tied to each of the cords of the lash leaves its mark. The crowd, hot, angry, loud, are turning against the one they recently hailed as their King! Above the crown of thorns is the sign authorized by Pilate written in Hebrew, Greek and Latin, "This is Jesus of Nazareth, King of the Jews." The Mother, grieving. The darkened sky. The repentant thief. Christ's last words. The temple curtain ripped apart signalling the end of an era.

'A Doctor at Calvary,' published in 1950 by Dr. Pierre Barbet, a surgeon, examines in a scientific way the four Gospel accounts, the known execution customs of a crucifixion, and the markings on the Shroud of Turin. As a forensic pathologist, the author describes some of the mysterious happenings during that gruesome torture and explains details in a factual, unemotional way. Roman justice called for either the lash *or* execution. Jesus was condemned to both.

Death came slowly, by asphyxiation, as the prisoner's strength weakened. The condemned man had to pull himself up every time he needed to take a breath. It was agonizing to lift himself up from the hanging position when he could rest, and bear his weight on the spikes gouging through his wrists and feet. After as much as three days of exposure, the criminal was exhausted and could no longer draw breath.

Because Jesus' execution was begun just before the Sabbath, and evening was approaching, the order was given to speed the death of the two other criminals. Their legs were broken, so they would be dead and buried before sunset. Jesus had already given up His spirit, so, like the Passover lamb, His bones were not broken.

Just to be sure He was dead, one soldier rammed his spear into Jesus' side. Blood and water flowed. The author, as a doctor, verified that because of the extreme position of the victim, a clear liquid would have pooled around the heart. The details were accurately recorded in the Gospels which declare that 'blood and water' drained from Jesus' side.

It is gruesome to read, yet fascinating to understand how the physical facts confirm the Gospel account.

I also have a short article written by a modern lawyer trying to disprove the Gospels. He examined the Scriptures as if it were a legal case. Jewish Law forbade three particulars of this sequence. 1) a night trial, 2) condemnation immediately after sentencing and 3) capital punishment during Passover. It is also a noteworthy contradiction that the Temple authorities actually requested the death sentence for one of their own countrymen by the authority of their Roman oppressors.

The third book is one of many written about 'The Shroud of Turin' which is believed to be the actual burial shroud of Jesus that was found in the empty tomb after the Resurrection. Although early legends cannot be verified, the linen cloth has been carefully preserved in a chapel in Turin, Italy, since the late 1300s. The linen has been repaired after being scorched by fire and damaged by water. For centuries, the brownish markings on the cloth in the shape of a man were blurry and hard to understand. In 1898, with the invention of cameras, the photographic negative showed much more detail. More recently, scientists have been permitted to make a close examination and perform various tests to determine the authenticity of the artifact. No forgery method has come close to producing a similar image on similar cloth. Art historians believe that details that can be seen in many portraits depicting Jesus can be traced back to the image of the face on the Shroud of Turin.

Good Friday

Mass is at 3:00pm.

I arrive early and silently pray the Sorrowful Mysteries of the Rosary, each scene is vividly reenacted in my imagination.

I also want to spend time appreciating the fourteen woodwork pieces which convey the Stations of the Cross. Carved by a local artist, these portraits are unusual because the closeup point of view brings the observer into the scene instead of standing back to see the entire panorama.

Only Pilate's hands are in the basin, trying to wash away the responsibility. Only Jesus' hands lift the massive, heavy beam. Only the back of His head, down on the rocky road, after He fell. Only Jesus' open, innocent hand beneath the soldier's left hand setting the spike, his right hand poised to strike the hammer's first blow. Only His bowed head crowned with thorns. Only the grieving hands of friends, rolling the heavy stone to close the tomb.

Quietly, Mass begins. Once each year, the priest wears a black robe, prays prostrate and leads the faithful in the Veneration of the Cross.

It would be impossible to comprehend the meaning if I was merely standing to the side, watching. By participating in these rituals, I am overwhelmed with emotions, insights and deeper understanding.

Saturday

I spend the day at the church, in the meeting room downstairs, working on a project at the table. I brought my new Bible and a book containing the readings for Mass for all three Liturgical Years, as well as the Breviary. I want to mark in the Bible all of the passages that are used and the time of year they are read. I also mark Psalms and other places in Scripture that I know as songs. It is a quiet day. There is much to reflect on.

A lengthy nighttime Mass is traditional today. The priest wears white. Candles and an outside fire are part of the ceremony. A sequence of readings reminds us of the Good News. "This is the night when Jesus Christ broke the chains of death and rose triumphant from the grave!"

The Creation story is read. Then the call of Abraham. Next the Exodus is declared. Then powerful passages from the prophets Isaiah, Baruch, and Ezekiel. In-between each reading, a Psalm pointing to the Messiah is sung. A brief Epistle, then the Gospel of the Easter morning gladness completes the Liturgy of the Word.

The Sacraments of Baptism and the Eucharist follow. Now they are even more deeply meaningful to me as I realize anew the continuity of the God's Salvation Plan from the beginning of time.

Some continue in prayer all night.

I return to my lodging, and wait in the lobby for the bus to leave at 11:30pm.

I arrive home in the wee hours. My heart is buoyant. I am so glad I did this. Am I asleep? I seem to hear the music, the chants, the prayers.

Sunday

I come home so that I can prepare a Sunday School project for the children in Blue River on this beautiful Easter morning. Like a cartoon strip, I have drawn little figures with captions so the children can remember and retell the story of Jesus from Good Friday to Easter morning.

When I phone my Mother to share my experiences, she tells me something about my life that I did not know. I was baptized as an infant on Easter Sunday. Long ago I wore the white dress she stitched by hand.

My story is a thread woven into this tapestry.

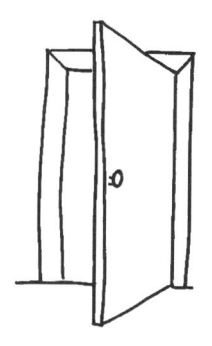

Chapter 10
Friday, February 9, 2018

> Undertake difficult tasks
> by approaching what is easy in them.
> Do great deeds
> by focusing on their minute aspects.
> —*Tao*

↘↓↙

This is my situation.

I am writing about today, while it is still today. Very unusual. Even in my journal (which I do first thing in the morning) I write about the past, yesterday, because nothing has happened yet today. I seem to need time for swirling emotions to settle and take meaning, for mixtures of experiences to distill into words, for my mind to be able to construct sentences.

So. Here I am. Today.

This winter is much the same, and yet, entirely different from previous Februaries. Here is a comparison.

Usually, I cheer myself up and make plans. But then I have to cancel. I am so frustrated and disappointed when the winter weather blocks safe travel. It is 45 miles to town with very few houses along the way. Black ice, slushy ruts, or new snow, are all too hazardous for me to drive the distance alone. To prevent the unpleasant cycle of hopeful anticipation followed by discouragement, I made a decision this winter not to go out on the highway at all. I am not even going to try to go to choir practice, make appointments, attend meetings, volunteer at school or prepare lessons for the children at church. I decided not to even try to go anywhere at all for Christmas. Except brief grocery runs with my husband in our 4x4, I have not been to town at all this winter.

But now, this year, I am surprised! I do not feel the stress. I don't need to ask my husband to look at the weather reports or listen to the truck drivers to try to find out, "How are the roads?" I am not getting my hopes 'up,' nor do I experience the usual 'down' of the heavy disappointment when I have to cancel.

Usually, I choose long term sewing projects for the winter to keep myself occupied. I use materials I have collected and stashed and hoarded. A colourful mess of fabric spills all over the living room floor. I use the fun of creativity to shield myself from the isolation. No clear roads equals no shopping for me!

Usually, quilting is a favourite. Mending takes days. When I cut up old t-shirts, I can braid rugs. When I cut up old jeans, I can invent denim projects.

But now, this year, at long last, I have come to the realization that my children are not ever going to come back to use their rooms. Clearly, the time I gave them and the space they needed are now my own to use as I desire. And so, as if I have been given an entirely new lifestyle, I have identified three new goals.

1) Clear out one room upstairs and re-purpose it as a Studio. How marvellous!

2) Write Book 3 together with Book 4 of my memoir series. Sounds like fun.

3) In order to both clear out the studio room and find clues to write about, I have brought 10 boxes of paper downstairs to sort through. Ugh! This one is hard to do.

↘↓↙

Studio

Usually, in February, 'I wish I was someplace else.' Like Dorothy, I yearn for 'somewhere over the rainbow.' Every avenue seems to be a dead end. Limitations rule my life.

But now, this year, I am trying to change my mind. Like Dorothy I have come to the conclusion, 'There's no place like home.' If I focus and visualize what I wish for, I can make 'this' be 'the place' I want to be. Focus. Make a plan. Take action. Get results. Change my environment.

So? What do I wish for?

My new Studio will be for movement, and music, and fitness, for sewing, and spinning wool, and craft projects. I may not be with other people for these 100 days, but, I can still do the things I love most. So, on December 23, when we made one last trip to town, I bought a gallon of pale yellow paint!

"Who buys paint just before Christmas?" I overheard the sales lady mutter.

"I do!" I eagerly grinned.

It was a great Christmas project!

First: I emptied the room. Then: I painted. Next: Kevin and I laid laminate flooring. After that: I returned book shelves, a cupboard and counter top, table, desk and bench, tape deck and CDs, tubs of fabric and the sewing machine, guitar and music stand. Kevin installed a mirror and ballet barre! I refreshed the books and supplies, weeded out what was unnecessary and filled my car with a load for the Thrift Store. My goal is not to save things 'from the past,' but rather, have available things I need 'for the future.'

↘↓↙

Write

Usually, I scribble in a Journal almost every day. It has no formal purpose. It's like looking in the mirror. Hello? Am I still here?

But now, this year, like a hot air balloon, I know that my writing does accomplish something. I am an author! I have sold over 1000 books! Feedback has been very encouraging. People like to read the words I choose! People like the stories I share! I certainly don't feel so alone when I get a royalties cheque in the mail for books sold in a city far away!

Usually, I write an 800 word 'Reflections' column every two weeks, send it by email, and eagerly read my bimonthly compositions in 'The Valley Sentinel'[21] newspaper from Valemount (90 miles to the north). Or, I write a 350 word news or opinion piece, or a 700 word 'Valley Voices' history column for 'The Clearwater Times'[22] newspaper 45 miles to the south. I have been earning a little spending money by writing since 1986.

But now, this year, I am trudging ahead, typing out the first draft of '10 Days in February' as well as '10 Days in March.' Aesop's Fables come to mind. I am the tortoise. Slow and steady. I am using the same method I started out with when I wrote Book 1, '10 Days in December.' I spend a whole day to write a chapter, print it, then mail it to my Mother. It is encouraging, in these long months of isolation, to know that there is an audience out there.

Friday, February 9, 2018

Right now, while I write, it is February. Some things do not change. The sky is grey. The highway is icy. My life becomes very small. It is still hard to face another day of February.

But now, this February, I notice that some things have changed. My newlywed 'dream' of life in a log cabin in the mountains has indeed come true. It is now forty years after we began. I am not cold. I have electric light, washer, dryer, stove, TV, computer. I have a telephone. My woodshed is full. My freezer, root cellar and pantry are well supplied. Our vehicle runs. My children are grown and gone. My husband is retired. Home. Safe. In fact, right now, he just finished doing the dishes while I peck away at the keyboard.

I think this will be what I write about. Today. Yes. The present time will be the last chapter of the '10 Days in February' book.

↘↓↙

Papers

Going through these ten boxes of paper is going to be overwhelming. Will I really throw away Christmas letters? Family photos? My own children's school papers?

Intensely, I want to to hold on. Why? I search inside. Do I really need this acknowledgment that I achieved so much? Nobody saw me do it. Nobody saw the preschool, the Sunday School, the Brownies, the library volunteering, the homeschooling projects. Back then, there was no requirement that there would be two adults present when working with children. I did it alone.

There was no extended family near by. Nobody except Kevin and I saw these four children grow, learn, produce creative inventions, funny dress-up parties, naughty lies, sick or injured, exploring the mountains, building with Lego, working in the garden. And how often was he at work and I was the only witness to a significant moment of family history?

If I burn these papers, will that mean I do not value all of this? What can I do to make it OK to let go?

I switched gears yesterday. Zero writing. I started sorting papers and spent twelve hours hunched over the stack of boxes. When it got dark, Kevin and I went outside and burned the boxes of discards, poking the layers with a long stick, watching the orange flames.

There go the brochures, magazines and newspapers I picked up in Brooklyn. Will I leave the Back-to-the-Land lifestyle? Will I pursue a career? Flames consume applications for university. Social Worker? Speech Therapist? Early Child Development professional? Coloured advertisements fade to black. No more posters announcing child-friendly events, library schedules, parenting information or support groups.

I decided not to pursue a career. I could not have known when I was eighteen years old that this topic that I love so much would open up to many professions. I lived in a time when it seemed like the only two roles for women were to be a stay-at-home-mom or to remain single and have a career. Traditional families raised their kids the same way they were raised. Nobody knew about child psychology. Nobody ran daycares or parent education groups.

I toss another load on the fire. Good-bye flip-chart pages that I prepared for the 'Chronic Disease Self-Management' seminars that Cheryl and I delivered.

I burned the hydro bills. After those five years living in the wilderness with kerosene lamps and flashlights, I am grateful every single day for electric lights. Kevin paid all of those bills with the sweat of his brow. I managed all the money. My handwriting is on every bill.

Friday, February 9, 2018

I burned the phone bills. Now there is no record of the frequent times I talked with my Mother, the precious times I phoned the kids away at school, me calling home 'collect' when I was on trips, Kevin calling me when he was on trips. All gone. It feels horrible.

I burned monthly bank statements. We no longer use the technology of writing on those yellow deposit slips, writing checks, mailing envelopes to pay bills on time, getting bank statements in the mail... all destroyed.

I burned the credit card bills. I felt ill as the familiar letter head caught the flame, shrivelled, crispy, black char melting into the snow. Those bills blaze a trail of trips. How did we pay the tuition for four children? How did we pay for four weddings? The credit card bills represent awkward arguments, Kevin's effort, my budgeting, occasional splurging, privately selfish, generous gifts, all recorded. All records gone.

I did decide to keep evidence that will help me prepare to write future books. And I retrieved quite a lot of unused paper, folders and other office and art supplies.

I have another box of old papers ready to burn. However, I feel ill deep in my heart.

I hesitate.

The box of papers I have ready to burn has Kevin's pay slips: years, and years, and years of pay slips. Elastic bands hold white paper, all folded, all in order. Each page records the hours he worked for his wife and children and home. He endured hardship outdoors, long hours, mean bosses, dangerous hazards, miserable co-workers. Am I really going to burn them? His rate of pay changed over the years. Will I discard all of that? He worked safely! He stayed healthy! He's home now! Retired! Many of his co-workers never made it to this moment. Am I going to disregard this achievement? Is it a celebration to burn this evidence of a life of dedication? For ten of his 33 years,

February Chapter 10

Kevin worked alone, patrolling at night on the train tracks. Who knew if he was asleep or on guard? Only his own conscience. Here is the stack of pay notices to prove he did it. And what does he have to show for it? A house. A wife. Kids grown and gone. The papers show the trail. They show the groceries and gas, the dentist and pharmacy, the clothing and shoes.

I can't decide what to do.

↘↓↙

Quietly, I check inside. Am I re-experiencing depression?

Usually, I dip down into a depression at some point during the winter months. Since 2010, I have attended the last of the weddings of our four children, passed through menopause, faced a cancer diagnosis, surgery and treatment, and entered a new chapter when Kevin took early retirement. Each change has made an impact on my well-being, but none have required antidepressant medication. I keep alert. I listen inside myself. But, I am OK. And grateful!

But now, this year, I ask myself, "Does February still feel like the longest month of the year?" I don't really have depression. I don't really 'wish I was someplace else.' I have much fewer limitations. But, I'm not exactly enthusiastic, either.

I am 60 years old now. I don't want to be a miserable old hag. I want to give up the struggle to find contentment. I ask myself, "Is everything significant that I have ever done all in the past?" I admire women who are older than me. They are active in choir, volunteer groups, extended family, travel to foreign shores, gain education, host events in the community, participate in various levels of government. I have some of these interests and skills, yet, for four months every year, I live in isolation. What can I accomplish? How can I participate? No place to go and nothing to do. Self-discipline, 'shoulds' and 'have-tos' are my theme song. An undercurrent of being mad at myself is a familiar 'go-to' position.

"I kind of wasted the day," I mumble to Kevin. "I didn't really accomplish much." I sigh.

Kevin points out a number of accomplishments. I seem to undervalue my own efforts.

However, over the years, I have developed and maintained healthy routines. If I get started, I can at least accomplish this much:

5:00-6:00: I wake up without an alarm clock.
Kettle for tea. Prayer book to read. Mass on TV.
Pen for the Journal.
Peek at my email and Facebook.
7:30: Max, our trusty yellow dog of fourteen years is gone. Now Shadow is my Personal Trainer. Outside I go tor 20 minutes to get my heart rate up.
8:00: I make breakfast with Kevin and plan food for the day.
10:00am-2:00pm: I like to focus and accomplish my writing, or sewing, or paper sorting.
2:00-6:00: Projects, or snooze, or phone calls, or return to clean up what I started.
6:00: Somehow, it gets to be evening, and my husband and I enjoy a TV movie date.
9:00: Bedtime.

I have always established routines to help me keep going. But it is so dreary. Some days I feel my toes and fingernails grip. Holding on the the earth. Holding on to my stamina. Holding on to a balanced sense of 'I'm OK.'

In January, I made a small quilt for a friend. Every two weeks, I have the newspaper articles to write. My husband's interests and comments make a small interruption through the fog in my mind.

I asked Kevin to set me up on the computer with Solitaire. Then I asked him to make it go away. Then I wanted it back.

Same with comfort food: brownies, and chocolate, and fried potatoes, and pasta. "Yes, please... I mean, No, thank-you.... wait... Yes, I do want some!" The bathroom scale knows the truth.

In my journal this morning, I explored the 'keeping' and the need to 'prove' that I made good decisions. Right now I have this 'standing on the edge of a cliff' feeling. The past has been destroyed. I can't go back. Only the wide, clear, vast future awaits. How do I know I will be OK?

I feel the same as on the day I buried Max. Gone. Fourteen years of my life are intertwined with a big yellow dog. Max. Nothing left. Just a rock over by the fir tree with his name and dates etched on it.

I also have five cases of photos to go through. Will I actually throw away any 'not good' photos? They are still holding tiny fragments of information. I'm afraid that I won't remember my own life if I toss them.

Ugh. I feel really heavy. Tears are close to the surface.

I guess it is a kind of grieving anytime you realize that each day is only one day and then it's gone.

The phone rang today. One of Kevin's railroad co-workers is gone. So many have died before they even reached their pension. I suppose we are entering the time of life when we will hear of friends, family, neighbours, movie stars and favourite musicians who have left their life on this Planet.

I walked to the post office today. I saw eight people I know! I mailed a parcel to our grandson. He lives in another country. Will he know who sent it? I got two cheques in the mail, both are payments for writing. That's a good thing. I have figured out how I can participate with the wider world through the internet.

I trudge home along the slippery road between the snowbanks pushed back like rugged mountains. I see the bald eagle that is frequently perched up high near the river's edge. The sun actually comes out. I feel its warmth on my back. Shadow wags her tail, glad to see me return. My husband and I watched a midday show we enjoy. The 2018 Winter Olympics opening ceremony is in four hours. I have supper planned. The laundry and floors and dishes are done.

Besides this inner thought process, that was my day.

Maybe, just maybe, it is the time in my life when I don't have to force myself to achieve, or measure my accomplishments, or try so hard to make an impression on the world. Maybe, just maybe, I have been running too hard, practicing a repeating loop of self-talk that sounds like perpetual disappointment. Discouraged. Never enough. Always one more thing. Sour.

Maybe, just maybe, the tune I could be playing in my head is 'Lucky Me!' I have an all expenses paid holiday in the mountains of British Columbia! Canada! People come from all over the world to enjoy this scenery. These snowy slopes. This clean air. This rushing flow of icy fresh water. This vast wilderness. Bald eagle sighting? For many people that is a once-in-a-life-time event! I get to see this mighty hunter nearly every morning!

My hubby willingly peels potatoes and we work together to make supper. I have many single friends. Others have husbands who are ill, or away, or loosing their memory, or simply distant.

↘↓↙

"Kevin, I want to tell you something." We two sit down for supper. "I didn't go jogging today. The ice is so smooth on our road that I went skating yesterday, but today, there is new snow, so I can't see where it is rough. I don't want to fall. I decided to clip on my cross-country skis." Kevin listens patiently.

"Left-right-left-right... I suddenly had an inspiration. In less time than it takes to tell, a flash of realization hit so forcefully I actually felt dizzy. The left side of my body is controlled by the right side of my brain. The right side of my body is controlled by the left side of my brain. Left brain is the logic and words and the 'male' characteristics. Right brain is the artistic, gestalt, the 'female' way of knowing and seeing the world." I summarize what I have read about.

Left-right-left-right. The flash was a synapse, a healing, an instant welding together and participation of both sides.

"Remember 'The Day on the Cliff'?[23] That day when I was eight years old? I was stunned. I could not obey my Father because that would be disobeying my Mother. If I obeyed my Mother, I would be disobeying my Father. I was paralyzed. He yelled at me. I have carried the confusion for so many years." Kevin is familiar with my life story.

"Then there were those other turning points," I continue. "You know the ones I mean. 'I want to be a minister'[24] and 'No, women cannot be ministers.' I have carried that confusion. I felt utterly stripped of wholeness. Self-doubt has been my constant companion." Kevin has heard all of this before.

"But, now: left-right-left-right... I have the realization that this is how much damage the old pain has caused. I am always mad at myself. If I clean the house, I think, 'I should have done work in the community.' If I volunteer, then I come home and say, 'This house is a mess.' If I read, or write, or learn, I think 'Why didn't I make anything?' or 'I never did any fitness today.' No matter what I pick, I am not doing the other thing. Locked into the unhappy scolding. Repeating this unpleasant cycle." But, this time, I have more to tell him.

Friday, February 9, 2018

"Left-right-left-right... What if 'I am I.' What if both the left *and* right, the Father *and* the Mother, the heart *and* the head, the logic *and* creativity are not one-or-the-other. What if one is not 'right' or 'better' and the other is 'wrong' or 'less.' What if *both* are important. What if I could go forward so that both components are not negating each other every moment? What if 'now' is good?"

I sit back, watching Kevin's face to see if he understands.

Husband and Wife. There is always more to learn about each other.

↘↓↙

All of this writing has certainly been therapeutic. All winter I have been returning to all of these memories and smoothing them out, finding words to describe my feelings and observations, fitting 'then' together with what I know 'now.'

I am not the only woman who has struggled to find a balance. Career? Home? I love to watch the 'Red Shoes' ballet movie,[25] although I always cry. The dancer is torn apart by the strain to chose between the joy of sharing her talent by performing on stage, and following her heart's desire to commit to the romance of marriage.

Can you have both?

I decided to be domestic. Therefore, I have very little to 'show for it.' No awards. No pay cheques. No properties, investments, educational credentials. No name on my office door.

Maybe my Dad was right, I should not have quit university.[26] Is there only regret now that I have more of my life behind me than ahead? Or, is there another way to see this part of the life cycle? Isn't the first priority in all parts of life to strive for 'contentment'? Is 'enough' actually 'enough'?

What Happened Next?

So, I guess I can sum up all of this rambling down to a few words: I am a holder-on-er. So many people say, 'Let it go!' I guess I don't! Is it holding me back? Am I less spiritual?

Holder-on-er. I think I made a new word. Sounds like 'honour.'

Yes! I want to honour the past. I love tradition. I want to pass on what I value to the next generation, to women younger than me. I want continuity in my own life. I don't want to destroy remnants of the past and forget. I want to recall, ponder, savour, fit the pieces together, retrace my steps, know the history of my own decisions. How did I get here? I want to be able to follow one long continuous thread, tracing my own Path that is my own life. Turning points and decisions, crossroads and hardship, doubt and clarity, cause and effect, purpose and effort, hypothesis and results, method and practice. No. I am not throwing everything away. I am not keeping every single thing, either. I am saving stepping stones. I am a quilter. I like fitting tiny scraps and little pieces into a beautiful pleasing whole.

Mortality. Legacy. Will anyone remember what I did with my time on Planet Earth?

Today I write. "I am here."
With my husband.
Twogether.
Twoday.

Chapter 10
Saturday, March 3, 2018

> I want to live. I want to grow.
> I want to see. I want to know.
> I want to share what I can give.
> I want to be. I want to live.
> —John Denver

↖↑↗

This is the last chapter!

The Grande Finale!

The exciting conclusion!

Wait. What? Was there a chase scene? A love scene? A hero? A mystery? Was there even a plot?

No.

But, that's OK because the purpose of a memoir is to 'preserve history through the eyes of those who lived it.'

And I did that. My own history, my dreams and goals, my family of origin, my marriage, my children, my neighbourhood, my wider world, my inner world, all sorts of ramblings are all preserved in nice tidy ink on paper.

And so, it is without apology for the lack of 'excitement' in my writing that today, Saturday, March 3, 2018, I wrap up my thoughts and write 'The End.'

↖↑↗

Today will probably be like every other day this winter.

The morning becomes just a little bit light, just a little bit before 6:00. I feed the fire, let out the dog, brew herbal tea, wrap up on my eiderdown robe, wool slippers and cozy blanket. I read my prayer book, scribble in my Journal, plan my day. I check my email, greet my husband, go outside. If the snow is deep, I can only walk on the paths or road. If there was a heavy snowfall during the night, it is too tiring to walk at all. If the plow truck scraped the snow away, there is ice so I can skate up and down the road. If there is a two-inch snowfall, I can go out on x-country skis. Two kilometres. That's it for me.

Bran muffin and yogourt, I still follow my homesteading diet. Lunch will be soup I make from the garden vegetables in the freezer. Supper will be local beef, with potatoes, kale, rhubarb and raspberries from our garden. It is satisfying to have these sunny summer resources through these long monotonous months.

"I'm going to work now," I kiss my husband and request that he not interrupt me for the next four hours, even though his desk is right beside mine. Type, type, type. Two finger pecking, pauses to go back with the spell check, pauses to search the thesaurus for the right word, pauses to dredge up the details from the depths of my memory. More tea. A dish of almonds. Type, type, type.

Saturday, March 3, 2018

I phone my Mother. "I have another chapter ready, I'll mail it tomorrow." I am so glad I have someone 'out there' to read these words I struggle so hard to compose. It will be months before the cases of books arrive, before I greet the smiling faces of fans, before I see cash in my hand, before I find cheques in the mailbox.

Drained, I somehow pass the afternoon. Hard to account for those hours. I can't seem to make any more decisions today. I start supper. Kevin has a favourite mystery show on TV. Then we watch a movie.

Sleep, or maybe laying awake, or reading in bed, or listening to a CD of quiet piano music, or battling old grudges, or finding a pleasant thought, the long dark night passes.

↖↑↗

What shall I write about today? I am so near the finish line, I can almost feel the ribbon across my chest, hear the cheers and reach for the trophy!

But, I have absolutely no idea how I will draw a conclusion from this jumble of memories. Yes, I had a theme, two themes actually. In February: depression. In March: volunteering. So? What is the sum total of these opposite experiences? What did I learn? How will the Reader benefit?

It was certainly satisfying for me to sort out, wrap words around and preserve these chapters of life. Perhaps others have travelled along similar Paths. Perhaps I have blazed a trail that younger Readers will find useful if they are faced with similar situations.

I can't think. I need to lie down. I doze off, pondering these last blank pages...

↖↑↗

"Kevin, please pass me some paper and a pen!" From previous experience, he knows that he mustn't ask questions when I get suddenly inspired. I scribble a list and draw a chart. The last chapter has arrived! "I did it! I'm done! I just have to expand the ideas on this chart into coherent sentences!"

"Good for you!" Kevin has been my champion supporter for all of these weeks. I have not carried in firewood from the woodshed, nor fetched potatoes from the root cellar, nor washed any dishes, nor looked after the dog. He has patiently endured my peck-peck-pecking on the keyboard and the silent distance between us while I am in focused concentration each day.

"Oh, I am so happy!" A weight has been lifted! I can see clearly! I am buoyant! I can feel the wind in my sails! The hot-air balloon is lifting! The sky is the limit!

So, here it is: the 'A-ha!' moment, slowly takes shape into English sentences to carry my thoughts to other minds and hearts.

↖↑↗

I realized three things in that flash of a moment.

First, and most significantly, the same things that made me so satisfied and happy in my early childhood actually match the dreams I have been striving for since I was a young bride.

Saturday, March 3, 2018

Childhood Enjoyment	Newlywed Dreams
music and dancing	get married
live in the mountains	go out west
read 'Little House' books	build a log cabin
care for my new baby sister	raise a family
go to Sunday School	teach our children about the Lord
participate in Brownies	volunteer in my community
learn about the authors Helen Keller and her teacher Annie Sullivan	then write a book about it

Secondly, I can now see why the disappointments are so painful and depression is so easy to slide into. Depression happens whenever there is a lack of these activities. No music? No dance? The silence is crushing. Trips to the city? I experience 'Culture Shock' and withdraw. Although the isolation of my mountain lifestyle can really bring intense loneliness through the winter, the 'homesteading' lifestyle also holds a great deal of satisfaction as the accomplishments and teamwork and 'do-it-yourself' home economics knit together in a wholesome way. No children? The empty nest is hard for my heart to cope with. No Sunday School? I feel like I am slowly suffocating. No volunteering? I don't know how to spend my time or organize my priorities and get lost in a foggy, boundary-less marsh. No writing? Without words, my mind becomes exhausted by a swirling confusion and aimless wandering.

Now the significance of these 'dreams' has become clear. My 'dreams' are not wafty imaginings. This is my core. My foundation. My fuel. My song. My life's breath. Although I have chosen a 'make do with less' lifestyle, I cannot ignore these sources of nourishment. These activities are not optional.

Thirdly, in a bold new way, I know I can sort out the feelings of depression if they ever come creeping back attempting to entangle my mind. The antidote to depression is reawakening my 'dreams.' I can be sure to provide for myself, not as a luxury, but as a necessity. I can funnel my resources, communicate with my husband, schedule outings and projects and friends. I can avoid things that mean less and provide for myself things that have more value.

No longer vague or wavering, I rededicate my efforts to seek ways to nourish my Heart, Spirit, Mind and Body with determination and purpose.

I can deliberately move towards and away from activities and people who bring the emotions: Glad, Sad, Mad, Afraid.

It is not OK to merely 'survive.' I can 'thrive'!

↖↑↗

What Happened Next?

Sunday: Glad!
Kevin and I braved the winter roads to attend Mass! I contacted the parents so that I could meet with the children before and after the service. It was so satisfying to prepare a lesson and a craft and listen to their questions and observations. Singing together! Familiar Scripture readings! My Heart opens wide to take in the recitations and prayers, and become revitalized by the meaning of the solemn ritual. The potluck luncheon afterwards was delicious, not only for my sense of smell and taste,

but also for my sense of belonging as I see and hear my friends and, of course, collect hugs!

Monday: Sad!

News arrived by email. Within a few days, there is expected to be a death in the family. A flurry of emails, travel arrangements across many time zones, outpouring of sympathy, encouragement, grief. Memories flood the mind. Emotions come in powerful waves. Suffering. Relief. Awareness of the uncertainty of each individual's life span. Could anything have been different? Prevented? Interventions. Decisions. And then: the last breath. The Body is empty. The Spirit is gone. Each family member has a different view of what is taking place. Is there life-after-death? Is there a Heaven? a Hell? Salvation? Based exactly on what? Is there reincarnation? Is death final? Is death a beginning? How do these beliefs play out during funeral preparations? How will this event impact family history? Family dynamics?

Also: Mad!

I try very hard to block this surprising emotion that tries to invade. My Mind is struggling like a drowning person with stormy waves crashing above and undercurrents tugging me down. Mad? Who do I have unfinished business with? What if I was the one on the death-bed? Who is mad at me? Why? What might I say or do to reconcile with this person? Who am I angry with? Is the grudge worth holding on to? What if there is no tomorrow? Will this 'Mad' block me from entering 'Eternal Rest'?

"Forgive us our trespasses as we forgive those who trespass against us..."

That is a rather weighty phrase. Can I forgive? Release?

Tuesday: Afraid!

Kevin and I make a scheduled trip to Kamloops for a necessary mammogram. As I climb the steep stairs towards the entrance of the hospital, panic comes over me. What has happened inside my body since the tiny spec of breast cancer was removed three years ago? Then, I calm myself with this thought. "The Lord already knows." The technicians will do their job. The Doctor will tell me the results of the test. I will step into a new chapter of my life.

'Tomorrow' is always unknown.

↖↑↗

I have learned a few things during this chapter of my life.

Balance:
Heart. Spirit. Mind. Body.
I need to attend to the nourishment of each.

Dreams:
Dreams become goals to guide me
as I make decisions and take action
so they will become reality.

Satisfactions:
I need to provide for the things
that have meaning and value in my life.

Emotions:
Glad. Sad. Mad. Afraid.
These will come and visit again and again,
and transition into other feelings,
like the weather or the seasons.

Saturday, March 3, 2018

I am married. I live in the mountains. My husband and I have finished raising our children and continue to enjoy the 'homesteading' lifestyle. Both of us volunteer. Music is part of my daily diet. I continue to write. Central to everything is this desire spoken of by the Psalmist.

> O give thanks unto the Lord, call upon His name,
> make known His deeds among the peoples!
> Sing to Him, sing praises to Him,
> tell of all His wonderful works!
> Psalm 105:2

↖↑↗

"Kevin?" I whisper, hoping he has not fallen asleep yet.
"Hmmm?"
"I can't think up an ending for my book. My life is still going. I can't write, 'The End.' I'm not finished living... or writing!"
No answer. Maybe he is asleep?
I often find the solutions to my problems as I pass through that magical moment of not-awake-not-asleep. That's why I keep a pencil and paper beside my bed.
And then, the idea arrives.
I will write, as Father Sasges used to say to me,
'To be continued.'
But, wait, Kevin and I are in this story twogether.
A new idea arrives.
I grab my pencil and paper and scribble the final words:
...Two be continued...

If you enjoyed
10 Days in February
and
10 Days in March
watch for future titles Eleanor Deckert is working on

10 Days in May... plant a seed and watch it grow

10 Days in June... one thousand dollars

10 Days in July... first fruits

10 Days in August... so many good-byes

10 Days in September... learning... teaching

10 Days in October... glad, sad, mad, afraid and thanksgiving

10 Days in November... maiden, mother, crone

Titles currently available through the Author's web page

www.eleanordeckert.com
also at Chapters/Indigo Bookstores

or order on-line from the publisher
books.friesenpress.com/store

Book 1 ~ 10 Days in December... where dreams meet reality

Book 2 ~ 10 Days in January... 1 Husband...
2 Brothers... 3 Sons... 4 Dads

Book 3 ~ 10 Days in February... Limitations

Book 4 ~ 10 Days in March... Possibilities

Book 3 & Book 4 in one volume

Book 5 ~ 10 Days in April... a detour through breast cancer

Endnotes

1. You can read the original 'Natural Life' magazine on-line. www.natural-lifemagazine.com/7810/NLO15. Our ad is on page 67, bottom left.

2. You can read the original 'Natural Life' magazine on-line. www.natural-lifemagazine.com/7810/NLO15. Our ad is on page 67, bottom left.

3. Read all about our wedding, trip out west, building the cabin and that first winter in 1978 in Book 1, '10 Days in December... where dreams meet reality' by, Eleanor Deckert, © Second Edition 2016, FriesenPress

4. See photos of how Kevin accomplished building the cabin in Book 1, "10 Days in December" chapter 3 of my web page. www.eleanordeckert.com

5. You can go to links on You Tube to enjoy the advertisements, theme music and watch episodes of these popular 1960s and 1970s and TV shows.

6. Book 1, '10 Days in December... where dreams meet reality' by, Eleanor Deckert, FriesenPress, Second Edition 2016, is available through my web site, www.eleanordeckert.com and as a hard cover, soft cover or e-book.

7. Stackwall is also called: cordwood masonry, stackwood, stovewood construction. There is lots of on-line info under these names. It was a very enjoyable way to build and we highly recommend it.

8. Read more about my family of origin in Book 2, '10 Days in January... 1 Husband... 2 Brothers... 3 Sons... 4 Dads' by, Eleanor Deckert © 2016, FriesenPress

9. I kept a Journal and I found these books helpful. 'Homecoming' by John Bradshaw, 'A Road Less Travelled' by M. Scott Peck, 'The Artist's Way' by Julie Cameron

10. clearwatertimes.com has a 'search' tool. If you type in 'Valley Voices: Eleanor Deckert' you can read over 20 history articles that I have written.

11 The description of this sad day is recorded in Book 2, '10 Days in January... 1 Husband... 2 Brothers... 3 Sons... 4 Dads' by, Eleanor Deckert © 2016, FriesenPress

12 More info about the Seer-Church teachings are found throughout Book 1 and Book 2.

13 'Seven Predictable Patterns'® seminars by Eleanor Deckert, will be the topic of one chapter in Book 7 '10 Days in June... one thousand dollars' and will be described in detail in the future Book 10 '10 Days in September... learning... teaching.'

14 My adventures as a Super Nanny will be the topic of one chapter in Book 7 '10 Days in June... one thousand dollars.'

15 On February 15, 2018, Charles Labun of the University of Victoria gave permission to quote from 'Living a Healthy Life with Chronic Conditions Self-Management Course, Leader's Manual,' © 1999, published by the University of Victoria, Centre on Aging, based on the work of Stanford Patient Education Research Centre, Palo Alto, CA.

16 See this 1965 school photo of eight-year-old Eleanor on the back cover of this book!

17 Jon Samson's songs are recorded on his CDs 'Kids Album,' 'Another Kids Album,' 'A New Kids Album,' available to purchase, or listen for free on Spotify, or search for 'Jon Samson' on You Tube to hear lots of his music and the way he works with children in therapy and as an entertainer. www.cocreativemusic.com

18 'Rome Sweet Home' and 'Hail, Holy Queen' by Scott Hahn as well as many of his lectures on CD from Lighthouse Catholic Media have helped me see the value of Catholic teachings and customs, Scripture study and traditions.

19 Search for 'Father Sasges' or 'Father Emil Sasges' for You Tube interview, magazine and newspaper articles, obituary. Alternative spelling 'Emile Sasges.' I wrote a 2-part 'Valley Voices' history piece for the 'North Thompson Times' newspaper.

20 This beautiful hymn is performed with a slide show on You Tube.

21 thevalleysentinel.com has a 'search' tool. If you type in my name, you can read lots of articles. Or contact me through Facebook. I am having the whole collection printed in a spiral-bound booklet.

22   clearwatertimes.com has a 'search' tool. If you type in 'Valley Voices: Eleanor Deckert' you can read over 20 history articles that I have written.

23   This frightening episode of my life is described in Chapter 1 of Book 2, '10 Days in January... 1 Husband... 2 Brothers... 3 Sons... 4 Dads.' by, Eleanor Deckert © 2016, FriesenPress.

24   This life-changing episode of my life is described in Chapter 4 of Book 1, '10 Days in December... where dreams meet reality' by, Eleanor Deckert © 2016, FriesenPress.

25   'The Red Shoes' 1948 ballet movie stars Moira Shearer. There is a new stage version choreographed by Matthew Bourne which premiered in London in 2016.

26   The whole conversation is in Chapter 10 of Book 1, '10 Days in December... where dreams meet reality' by, Eleanor Deckert © 2016, FriesenPress.

What Readers Are Saying

"When I read '10 Days in December,' I couldn't put it down. I just finished reading '10 Days in January.' When is your next book coming out?"
—**Dorothy, Foster Parent**

"Your books are very popular at the library and often requested."
—**Mike, Librarian**

"I read both of your books! They were featured in my book club!"
—**Brenda, Library Patron**

"Eleanor, it was such an experience reading your book. Again you swept me away with you and I felt like I was right there. It was absolutely fascinating."
—**Kathy, Social Worker**

"... heartwarming ... wholesome ... struggle ... peace ... crushing depression ... inspiration and comfort ... devotion to family ... rich and full ... simply golden ..."
—**Evaluation Editor, FriesenPress**

About The Author

> Think of everyone as a child
> in need of friendship and love.
> —John Bradshaw

Encouraged by reader feedback and her ever-expanding contacts through interviews, speaking engagements and book signing events, Eleanor Deckert spent the winter of 2017-2018 describing more personal details of her homesteading lifestyle, marriage and family, inner turmoil and satisfying volunteer projects.

"Much of my life is simply the 'Serenity Prayer.' The things that cannot change are the 'Limitations.' The things that can change are the 'Possibilities.' Although the isolation of the winter months still presses down on me," Eleanor explains, "I continue to explore creative opportunities and re-dedicate myself to volunteering in new and interesting ways."

Printed in Canada